"MiSS, I DON'T GiVE A SH*T"

<u>Two memories:</u>

Me around 8 years old: Mum, why is Laura always dirty and scruffy?

Mum: I think her family doesn't have much money; they can't buy as many clothes as we can.

Me: People pick on her, I tried to play with her, but she won't play nicely.

Mum: I don't think her family have been able to teach her how to do that, it must be harder for her mustn't it?

Mum – Alyson Bates

Dad to me, around 15 years old: Equal doesn't mean the same; I always mow the lawn, but your Mum remembers our pin numbers.

Dad – Anthony Bates

Thank you to my Mum and Dad, for giving Adam and I such a solid foundation from which to fly.

"MiSS, I DON'T GiVE A SH*T"

Engaging With Challenging Behaviour in Schools

Adele Bates

CORWIN

A SAGE Publishing Company

SAGE Publications Ltd
1 Oliver's Yard
55 City Road
London EC1Y 1SP

CORWIN
A SAGE company
2455 Teller Road
Thousand Oaks, California 91320
(0800)233-9936
www.corwin.com

SAGE Publications India Pvt Ltd
B 1/I 1 Mohan Cooperative Industrial Area
Mathura Road
New Delhi 110 044

SAGE Publications Asia-Pacific Pte Ltd
3 Church Street
#10-04 Samsung Hub
Singapore 049483

Editor: James Clark
Senior assistant editor: Diana Alves
Production editor: Katherine Haw
Copyeditor: Catja Pafort
Proofreader: Tom Bedford
Indexer: Charmian Parkin
Marketing manager: Dilhara Attygalle
Cover design: Wendy Scott
Typeset by: C&M Digitals (P) Ltd, Chennai, India
Printed in the UK

Library of Congress Control Number: 2021932748

British Library Cataloguing in Publication data

A catalogue record for this book is available from the British Library

ISBN 978-1-5297-3157-6
ISBN 978-1-5297-3156-9 (pbk)

At SAGE we take sustainability seriously. Most of our products are printed in the UK using responsibly sourced papers and boards. When we print overseas we ensure sustainable papers are used as measured by the PREPS grading system. We undertake an annual audit to monitor our sustainability.

TABLE OF CONTENTS

ABOUT THE AUTHOR

'I've had juice poured on my head, been whacked by a skateboard – and have taught a Year 7 pupil who has experienced severe trauma how to read their first ever word...'

Adele Bates is a Behaviour and Education Specialist who supports school leaders, classroom teachers, homeschooling carers, and parents to empower pupils with behavioural needs and Social, Emotional and Mental Health needs (SEMH) to thrive in their education. As well as enabling these pupils to learn their timetables or to pass an exam, her main ambition is to help these, often misunderstood, young people to be a part of positive social change. Part of that is advocating on their behalf in wider society, creating platforms for their voices to be heard and to be part of building an inclusive education system for all – hence why she's written this book.

Adele has nearly 20 years' teaching experience in a variety of settings: mainstream primary and secondary, Pupil Referral Units, Alternative Provision and Special Schools. She trains and mentors teachers and trainees and is a Behavioural Consultant for senior leaders and local authorities, advising on whole school approaches to supporting pupils with behavioural needs and SEMH.

In 2019, Adele was awarded a grant to carry out an educational research trip in Finland to observe, teach, interview and learn about the Finnish Education System's inclusive approach to education. This has informed her approaches since.

Adele is a TEDx Speaker 2020 and has delivered training and keynotes for educational events and organisations across Europe, including the National Education Union and Amnesty International Education. She is the Educational Associate for Trauma Inform, an Associate on Behaviour with Independent Thinking and has been interviewed as an expert on teenage behaviour for BBC Radio 4. Adele is a contributing writer for education books: *For Flourishing's Sake, Big Gay Adventures in Education, Square Peg* and *The Big Book of Whole School Wellbeing.* She has a First-Class Undergraduate Degree, a Master's Degree and a PGCE.

For Adele's tips, resources and to work with her further, visit her website at adelebateseducation.co.uk where you can also become a part of her community of Inspiring Educators. You can catch her on Twitter @adelebatesZ.

Adele is originally from Burton-on-Trent, now based in Brighton (and sometimes Bulgaria) where she lives with her partner Elitsa. Her brother Adam is usually floating around in her life too. Adele is a trained opera singer; she enjoys knitting, yoga, meditation, painting, flamenco, forests and never stops reading.

ACKNOWLEDGEMENTS

I must start with the brilliant story that brought this, my first book, into existence.

Rachel Musson, founder of Thoughtbox Education, had given me a free ticket for an education conference – despite never having met me. Rachel was one of the first people I didn't know who I spoke to about being a freelance educator. She was incredibly enthusiastic and invited me to do my first ever education interview as a blog post for her company.

At that conference, I wandered around the book stands in a break and, for some unplanned, unknown reason, got inspired to ask one of the chaps what you actually had to do to become an author. Publisher at SAGE & Corwin, James Clark, talked me through the proposal process and asked "why, do you have an idea?". Honestly, I had no idea, but having found out I was speaking to a publisher, I blagged something about a 'behaviour book'. James sounded vaguely interested. At that point I had noticed he had been multitasking: keeping watch on the stand, with watching the cricket on his iPad. I seized my opportunity and cheekily suggested that he go to my website and read my blog instead...

A couple of weeks later, I was astounded that James emailed me, having thoroughly read my blog, encouraging me to put forward a proposal. It was the end of summer term, Year 11 exam-madness, so I got a bit excited but had to put it off until we reached the holidays. At that point, I read the email properly and digested what this could mean – I could write a book. Gosh.

So firstly, thank you to Rachel for the free ticket to an event I otherwise wouldn't have gone to, and thank you to James for prizing himself away from the cricket on that sunny afternoon.

Once in the SAGE world, Diana Alves has given me ongoing encouragement from the start. Her positivity and eye for detail have been invaluable. I am also unsure how she manages to read and feedback on things so quickly when I'm having a 'writer's wobble'. Thank you.

At the very start of the process, I attended a fantastic course with Arvon, led expertly by Alexander Masters and Melissa Benn. Not ever having thought of myself as a writer before, this was the first writer's retreat I had ever been on; it was a dream come true. Thank you to all of the Arvon people who support writers in this way. It makes a huge difference. Melissa, thank you for mopping up the tears and helping me realise I could do this at the early stage when the shine of 'oh I'm writing a book!' turned into 'ummm...how do I write a book?' Your own writing in education is an inspiration. Also thank you to Prof Zoë Playdon, Debra Shaefer and the other supportive participants on the course; I can't wait to read your books too.

Next, I acknowledge my interviewees: when I had the idea of introducing experts for each chapter, I thought of my dream team – I got them. Some are brilliant friends and colleagues; others are people whose work I was admiring from afar. There were also a couple of people I was secretly fan girling inside and couldn't believe they said yes! So, for your time and enthusiasm for this project, and more importantly, for the work you do for our young people, thank you: soon-to-be Dr Frederika Roberts, Rachel W, soon-to-be Dr Lisa Cherry, Frédérique Lambrakis-Haddad, Kate McAllister, Mark Goodwin, Pranav Patel, Dr Emma Kell, Rachel Tomlinson and Bukky Yusuf.

Thank you to Elizabeth Wright for proofreading Chapter 7, to Anju Handa for creating a boundaries resource out of thin air for Inspiring Women Changemakers, *and* reading my conclusion and jumping on the phone at the eleventh hour on deadline day.

Along the way, thank you to cheerleaders: Jaime Jo Hallam, Apryl Simons, Barbra Dopfer, Alexandra Pope, Boris Angelov, Lucy Mott, Suzy Ashworth, Jamila Theobold, Dr Steve Roberts, George Gilchrist, Darren Abrahams, Vicky Tremain, Amber Kuileimailani Bonnici and people in the Inner Circle, for phone calls and messages of enthusiasm and encouragement throughout the writing process. Importantly, thank you to Amar Saggar for gifting me the all-important noticeboards that got me started off with the planning when all I had was blank pages; they helped a lot!

David Gumbrell is a new friend and colleague I made during writing, who helped with Chapter 9 via brilliant discussions, may this collaboration be fruitful and long. And thanks to Andy Taylor, aka @MrTs_NQTs for anticipating the synergy David and I would have in our work, making the introduction and trumpeting anything I write to his NQT gang.

Thank you to the Society of Authors for the Writers Grant during the unstable lockdown period. This enabled me to keep writing.

This book was written through many lockdowns both up a Bulgarian mountain (thanks to my hosts Laura Giosh-Markov and the tragically now passed away rock legend Konstantin Markov for the tranquillity, desk and raspberries) and in my Granny Pippa's house on our return to the UK. Thank you for the loan of your house Granny Pippa, Philippa Bates, it made a big difference in buying me time to finish writing. Moreover, thank you GP for your own lifelong advocation for education for all, it obviously rubbed off a bit.

Thank you to the many pupils and colleagues in different schools where I have worked. I cannot name all of you for safeguarding and practicality reasons, but you have helped me learn what I share now.

This book would not have been written, and definitely no one would have been interviewed, without my fabulous VA at the time Michelle Gillson. Thank you for keeping me in line and pointing out when I was being over-optimistic with my time-keeping. Best of luck in your business now as a Dubsado Expert...and thank you to my VA now Lora May for picking up so smoothly and cheerleading.

Ian Gilbert, a huge thank you for your proofreading and pushing me to claim *I am what I am* through my writing. Your support and provocation on the final push were invaluable – you made it a better book. I feel honoured to have had your expertise and guidance throughout this process, and it's a joy to be a part of the Independent Thinking family.

Mum and Dad Bates, Alyson and Tony, thank you for laying the foundations and supporting me in everything I do (even when you don't get it). Your unconditional love enables me to do the ambitious things I do.

Adam Bates, my baby brother, thank you for always being there no matter what, no matter when, and for never doubting my ability to do this, especially when I did. Hello?

Elitsa Zaykova, my unexpected, wonderful partner. Thank you for never questioning that I could write a book and never pretending you will ever read it. Your practical help – chef, IT support, finder-of-things-I-have-misplaced – and emotional support has enabled the book to get written. I love you.

Finally, thank you to Jemma King. On paper she is one of my proofreaders, but in reality, she has been the biggest advocator for this book from the start. A dear friend and excellent former teacher, who just happens to be a qualified proofreader, I could not have done this without you. You gave me an incredible blend of encouragement, brainstorming, heartstorming, thoughtful educational debate, listening, putting my inner critic in her place, comma placement suggestions, hours of your time, deep friendship, and of course, Menstrual Cycle Awareness. Thank you so much.

FOREWORD

BY BRITISH TEENAGERS IN ALTERNATIVE PROVISION FOR EDUCATION

I have written this book about young people for whom the education system does not work, and so I am honoured to have collated a foreword written by some of these pupils.

For confidentiality and safeguarding reasons, they must be kept completely anonymous. Some of these young people are in care, some have been excluded from mainstream schools, some excluded from several. All of them are of secondary school age and are now educated in Alternative Provision; this can range from PRUs to APs, some mainstream and some alternative or tutoring.

The young people were asked several questions, I have left their answers as raw and honest as I can, without my interpretation or advice for teachers on 'what you could do next' (there's plenty of that in the book).

Not all pupils were able to answer every question and some answers were too identifying to include. For me, the responses give us a huge insight into the educational journey and relationship that these young people form with schools in their childhoods. It makes me sad, angry and fuels me to do the work I do.

Please read their experiences, ideas and advice carefully. These young people, the ones whose behaviour has not been supported in our mainstream education system, are the experts after all.

It may be the most useful part of the book.

WHAT'S YOUR CURRENT SCHOOLING SITUATION?

"I've been to four schools, three primary and one high school. I'm currently in Year 8 but not in school. The plan is to start back at school in Year 9."

"Permanent exclusion, currently out of PRU."

"Two schools, one primary and one high school; hate both."

"Excluded several times from primary. One full time education so far at high school."

WHEN YOU HEAR THE WORDS 'SCHOOL' OR 'EDUCATION' WHAT DO YOU THINK OF?

"Frustrating, hassle, obligation, boring, rubbish; don't like it."

"Frustrating (enjoyable when I was doing what I wanted)."

"Hassle, stress, 'blags my head'. School is only fun when I am on the terror. Don't like it; crap."

"Community, opportunity, obligation, varied."

"Boring, but fun at the same time. I was actually quite good at PE, believe it or not. I was quite fit for a 6-year-old but not now. I loved break and lunch but the food could've been better."

DESCRIBE YOUR BEST TEACHER – WHAT MADE THEM SO GOOD?

"I either like a teacher or I don't, nothing in between. No reason either way. The day I understand why is the day I become a millionaire, but that will never happen anyway. Same for worst teacher, don't know really. Probably Miss P getting angry over the smallest thing, she needed to chill out, I can just rub the mistake out!"

"Nothing. Only thing was Forest School in Year 7, he let me plant and grow. We got wood and built a fire. He didn't boss me around, he wasn't trying to get me to kick off at him. Boxing was OK too."

"Only one at high school. Strict but liked him, sounds nice. He was in the army but he is funny sometimes. I liked Miss L at primary, not boring, she was funny and did fun things with the class. She explained things quickly, she was nice. Sometimes she shouted but we still got hot choc."

DESCRIBE YOUR WORST TEACHER – WHAT DID THEY GET WRONG?

"Teacher at high school, tells everybody off, you get an 'unmet' for anything, nearly every kid all the time. She has a weird way of saying 'Excuse me…'. She tells me not to jump around. This is annoying."

"Scottish teacher at high school, couldn't understand him. Gave detentions for anything, even your collar sticking up. Rules all the time, just a twat… did not like him."

"Maths at the PRU, always having a go. Picked on me, shouted at me that I was going to do some work today. Blagging me, threatened to take away the pool table for lunch if I didn't do the work. Kept shouting at me to do the work, I refused and he told me to get out. I carried on arguing and he grabbed me and tried to throw me out, we ended up on the floor. All the other kids were shouting and other teachers came. It wasn't just me, he spoke to all kids bad. He works at the high school now and he goes on about me to my mates and girlfriend – 'I don't care who your boyfriend is...'"

"I wish he didn't start it, he always was trying to wind me up. I didn't know what to do most of the time in lessons so why didn't he help me?"

DESCRIBE YOUR FAVOURITE MEMORY FROM ANY SCHOOL OR TUTORING – WHAT WAS SO GOOD ABOUT IT?

"Playing football on the field. I was good!"

"I liked playing rugby for the school team in Year 7. We won a couple of games. Me and R scissor tackled one of the other team, nearly broke him in half. I played second row."

"I went to C primary school from reception to Year 3. This is my favourite school because it is the one I have the most memories from, mainly all the people I knew there."

"Maths tests, I love them. I love being a geek and a nerd. It is not a contradiction. I loved getting a hot chocolate at primary."

DESCRIBE YOUR WORST MEMORY FROM ANY SCHOOL OR TUTORING – WHAT WAS SO BAD ABOUT IT?

"I hated the lessons and the teachers. On the last day I hit my mate with a tennis racket – I didn't hurt him and we are mates now. The school felt like high school, teachers were really strict and everybody hates them; most kids hated the lessons too. It was all points, teams and houses. Classes got split up and we were put into sets, I found myself with kids I didn't like. Plus, I got a detention for putting the date wrong – what was the big deal? I could have just rubbed it out. Also, I got an injury on my finger (some sort of callous or growth?) and it made writing hard, sometimes it was bleeding and I couldn't stop it. I had an operation to remove it in the end.

All that happened at school was I got told off for my finger bleeding on my work or not being able to write properly."

"I went to go on a managed move before I went to the PRU. Mom said I had to behave really well and keep quiet, don't mouth off. So I went into the meeting with the Headteacher and the Deputy and kept quiet. So the Deputy started saying he could tell how naughty I was just by looking at me. I didn't even say thank you when he opened the door for me, I said I was trying to keep quiet and they don't know anything about what I am like. I walked out of the office and didn't go on a managed move. It really blags my head when teachers do that, they shouldn't be allowed to do it."

"Detentions at high school... but these were kind of fun too."

IF YOU WERE TO BE ASKED HOW BEHAVIOUR SHOULD BE APPROACHED IN SCHOOLS, WHAT WOULD BE YOUR ADVICE?

"Rules: yes you need them, but kids don't follow them anyhow.

Punishment: doesn't work. I will do the thing I'm being punished for even more just to annoy teachers.

Rewards: these are good. I like to get something for being good.

Exclusion: Waste of time, I just get time to myself. No, I don't do the work..."

"They should believe kids more."

"Tutor is the best school I've had. Do small bits at a time – no orders or detention or stay behind. Much better away from my mates, not so good if my mates are around."

"Be chill with the kids. Let them take their time, don't rush work. Be calm, don't shout if they get it wrong!

Rules are OK for getting work but don't see why there are rules for tie, uniform, trainers; what's the point about rules for hair?

If I had a bad day I just want to go home and sleep; listen to music or video on my phone. But my bike is the best thing, it means everything to me and I wouldn't change it for anything.

I wish school didn't keep checking up on me when I was in school, every lesson somebody sticking their head in and asking if I was OK."

"Rewards are good for making me behave better – I can show my carer and make her proud.

Punishment doesn't work, I keep doing it. I get distracted and don't think of the consequences, I forget."

IF YOU HAD 2 MINUTES TO TELL ALL TEACHERS IN THE UK ONE THING TO MAKE THEM BETTER TEACHERS, WHAT WOULD IT BE?

"When you are telling kids off let them say their side too, don't cut them off."

"My message would be to *be fair*. Think about if a teacher was speaking to their own kids like that – they wouldn't like it. You are twice my age, why are you shouting at me? Blags my head."

"Make it better. Let me chew gum, it will help me focus and you wouldn't get a stupid black market in chewing gum where I pay 25p for one piece."

"My advice for teachers is don't be a twat or a dick."

OTHER COMMENTS?

"I don't really want to talk about school anymore…"

INTRODUCTION

"Miss, I don't give a shit."

"I cannot be arsed."

"Sir, you can just f*** off."

"Leave me alone…"

…and various other sweet refrains can be heard regularly up and down the country from pupils who are struggling to conform to our mainstream way of education. When you are the day-to-day teacher, Teaching Assistant, pastoral staff, senior leadership team, it is easy to be worn down or become numb to this kind of rhetoric and its associated behaviours.

These pupils are communicating to us a resounding "No." A no to the moment, to the work, to the lesson, to a peer, to the teacher, to education – or for some it's a much bigger picture; they are also saying no to mental health issues, learning difficulties, difficult home lives, past or current trauma, abuse or neglect. Most concerningly, some are saying no to themselves – the outward aggression is a façade masking an inner no: self-loathing, self-frustration, self-anger and fear.

"Miss, I don't give a shit" – what is this really communicating to us?

"Miss, leave me alone, I can't read and I'm embarrassed."

"Miss, I don't want you to care, because adults who care eventually leave me – that hurts."

"Miss, I'm scared to try in case I fail; when I fail at things I get punished or I need to punish myself."

"Miss, don't come too close – there's bad things I have to keep a secret from you."

"Miss, don't focus on me too much, you will discover I'm not worth it."

There are as many explanations as there are pupils – and remember, just because a kid does not have a label, doesn't mean there is 100% no needs.

Should this type of language, and associated behaviour, be punished? Should there always be consequences? Yes. And no.

Context is everything.

This book guides you through these very real conundrums, providing strategies that sit within your school's behaviour frameworks – whilst making a longer, and arguably much more useful, impact for learning, pupil wellbeing and sometimes safety.

WHY READ THIS BOOK?

Firstly, there are many practical tips, approaches and strategies that, if implemented (more on that in a moment), will help you and your staff to support the behavioural needs of even the trickiest "cherubs" in your classrooms and schools.

But that's just the surface.

This book is part of a much wider vision and movement. Particularly in the British education system in the past twenty years or so, there has been an increasing focus in our schools on teaching to the test, grades, performance-related pay for teachers, 'cracking down' on behaviour and expecting all our pupils to achieve the same things in the same ways. This takes us far; we have record high numbers of pupils reaching Further Education, which as a nation enables us to be one of the main economic and political players in industries worldwide – and if that's your measurement of success value, that's a good thing.

However, there is another side too. Thirty-five pupils a day are being excluded from our schools, illegal off-rolling is common place, as is advising parents and carers to homeschool pupils with certain needs as it's 'for the best' – without addressing for whom it is best (Henshaw, 2017).

Here are some statistics from the Making the Difference (Gill et al., 2017) exclusion report:

- It is our most vulnerable pupils who get excluded; they are twice as likely to be in care, four times more likely to have grown up in poverty, seven times more likely to have a special educational need and ten times more likely to suffer recognised mental health problems.
- Once a pupil is excluded they cost society £370,000 due to poorer outcomes.
- Once a pupil is put into Alternative Provision (AP) or a Pupil Referral Unit (PRU) they are less likely to be taught by qualified, consistent staff and are less likely to attain 5 GCSEs.
- In addition, one of the top reasons that teachers leave the profession is linked to challenging behaviour. Interestingly, in 2019 Jane Perryman and Graham Calvert discovered that it is not the pupil's behaviour per se that causes teachers to leave, but the lack of support teachers feel they have in coping with it (Perryman and Calvert, 2020), which we also address in this book.

These pupils, however, are not just a small part of a negative, media grabbing statistic. They are humans who have the ability to connect, learn and thrive, once the opportunity presents itself to them in a way they can safely take it.

My vision for education is one in which all differences are included and welcomed; an education which is flexible, relevant and leads towards positive social change.

This is at the heart of what this book is about. I believe that pupils with behavioural needs, who challenge the adults around them, have the potential to not just learn their timestables or get a GCSE, but to be key players in the social positive change our society so clearly requires; those key players could be widely known policy makers shifting nationwide infrastructure, or they could be the volunteer at the Citizens Advice Bureau (CAB) who supports a young person from attempted suicide to find the support they need. I know this to be true because I have the honour of knowing adults who have come on this transformational journey themselves, some of whom you will meet in the interviews accompanying each chapter.

And this is where we, the educators of the young people, come in. We may feel sometimes that what we do with our pupils is small and insignificant, and yet we have the position, power and therefore responsibility to positively influence our micro-communities. Sometimes it can feel like you're a mere cog in a machine with no agency; that a government, a curriculum or an inspection body are what dictate who you are as an educator and how you should teach – that is not the case.

What we do in our classrooms – virtual, remote, physical or otherwise – on a micro level makes a difference. The community we create in our schools can be the difference between safely belonging and thriving for a pupil – or being excluded, lost in the system and becoming one of those negative statistics.

How we relate to our pupils, the relationships we build, makes a difference to their lives.

You have that influence. *You* have that position of power and the responsibility to look after that most valuable resource in all of this – *you*. It's not a coincidence that this is where we begin in Chapter 1. In addition, over the year I took to write this book and interview the experts, I discovered an overriding theme from all of them: no matter which aspect of supporting behaviour we were discussing, self-care and reflection for the adults need to come first.

Yes, this book is a practical how-to in many ways. My desire, however, is that it is also a space to dream and connect with a wider vision of what education *could* be for all and realise what those first steps to that place might be for you, tomorrow morning, starting with the delightful 9F2 in the temporary mobile building with broken heating.

I address the people in my community as Inspiring Educators, because you are the ones in the classrooms and the schools and you *do* have the opportunity to inspire every day – which makes a difference to your pupils. This book tackles the moments when you feel less than inspiring, in fact sometimes when you feel totally hopeless. It provides a safe space for you to unpick some of the most challenging aspects of your job, connect with other stories and people who have similar experiences and, I hope, empower you to take the next step forwards.

HOW TO GET THE MOST OUT OF THIS BOOK

If you are like me, no matter what I say here, you will read this book cover to cover, take notes (in pencil, *never ink*) and try to apply everything.

Truly, this book can be approached in many different ways. One of my favourite chapters to write was Chapter 10: Troubleshooting, which gives you 'quick' answers to emergency questions, signposting to the relevant chapters and sections that will help you out – because I am fully aware that sometimes you don't need theory and reflection, you need something to put in place three lessons ago.

Aside from that, the *best* way to get the most out of this book is to implement, experiment, adapt and try again. Some of the approaches and strategies offered here you will have seen before. Some you will have tried before, and they will have failed. So why would you bother again? Because the joy and infuriation about supporting positive behaviour (and teaching in general), is that it is always changing. We need as big a toolbox as we can, because we never know when we will need to pick up that old spanner again, or try a shiny new jigsaw that we thought was too new-fangled for us – because it happens to be *the* tool that helps *that* pupil unlock their potential for learning in your subject.

Overall, keep asking questions: "Yes, I tried that with Year 11 last year, why didn't it work? How long did I try it for? What about it didn't fit for them? What could work better next year? How are these Year 11s different to last year's? How am I different? What have I learnt that means I now have different ways of using my tools? What has happened in the context of our community that has affected education?".

THE BIG BEHAVIOUR RULE

You will very rarely hear me discuss rules. Here's about the only one I share with everyone who works with me:

THE BIG BEHAVIOUR RULE

Any advice you receive from any well-meaning:

- Teacher
- Headteacher
- Specialist (including me!)
- Parent
- Carer
- Grandparent
- Politician
- Therapist

- Twitter feed
- Blog post
- School gates conversation etc.

you can override if it does not work for *your* pupil(s).

Because you are the experts on your pupils, your classroom, your school, your community and yourself. Whilst I or anyone else *may* have more experience or have read more books, we don't know exactly what it's like to be in your shoes – your job is to take any advice you receive and find out what works.

TRIGGERS

You have picked up a book with a swear word in the title, so I will assume that the odd curse will not offend you. In addition, there is content that touches upon traumatic and potentially upsetting experiences for some. It is vital that these are a part of the conversation about behaviour in schools and the point of including them is to investigate how you might support such a pupil who has these experiences, but please do look after yourself first.

SAFEGUARDING

Schools play an essential part in keeping our young people safe. Whilst reading this book it may prompt you into concerns over a pupil as you consider their situations and behaviour in different ways. I implore you to pass on concerns. All schools in the UK will have a Safeguarding policy, procedure and Safeguarding lead – find out yours. The best Safeguarding advice I have ever received was from Rachel W (Chapter 2), who told me: if it doesn't feel right, even if you can't explain it fully, tell someone, it could make all the difference to keeping a young person safe.

CHAPTER HEADINGS

Each of the "Miss" quotes from the chapter headings are real quotes that pupils have said to me over the years. As is the title of the book.

#INSULTOFTHEWEEK

At the start of each chapter, I share some of my favourite #InsultOfTheWeek quotes from my pupils. I have been sharing these with my community of Inspiring Educators for a couple of years now, many others have got involved – bringing much hilarity and reality checks when needed. We'd love you to jump on twitter with the hashtag #InsultOfTheWeek or contact me and share yours too.

ACTION BOXES

At the end of each chapter there is an action box outlining practical ideas for you to implement – next lesson, next week and long term. These, and your own variation of them, will be what transforms this process from reading a book, into making a positive difference to some of the most vulnerable pupils in your classroom.

A NOTE ON TERMINOLOGY

There is no perfect umbrella term to discuss the kind of pupils I wrote this book for – because they are all individuals and umbrella terms tend to exclude and mislabel. Most often I refer to 'behaviour that challenges the adults' because this behaviour can come from anywhere (other staff sometimes too) and the behaviour is not intrinsically linked to any person.

There is a glossary at the back explaining some common acronyms and terms used.

OTHER USEFUL POINTS

- Have a notepad and pen (or your digital equivalent) available for exercises, questions and reflections.
- When I ask you to "choose one-to-two pupils" in a thought experiment or activity, don't be tempted to think of your whole class or all of your SEMH pupils. I am specific for a reason – it is this specificity that will enable you to create *real* differentiation. The process of going through the activity with only particular pupils in mind will be so revealing you won't be able to help yourself but do the process again for all of them, once you see the effect your small changes are making.

ENJOY

I am a big advocator of enjoyment. You are investing your time and energy in this book, so make it as enjoyable as you can for you – a snippet over breakfast each morning, read it on the commute or form a book club and read it with others. The chapters can easily become bitesize for discussion groups – and for putting into action.

Make it work for you.

And finally, I would love to hear how you get on. I want to know what rings your bells, what made you think, what finally clicked into place for Mo in the behaviour unit in Year 7, what challenges you still face and how I can further support you to clear blocks and empower the young people in your care.

You can connect with me:
on Twitter at: @adelebatesZ
on LinkedIn at: www.linkedin.com/in/adele-bates-03b566208/
or on my website at adelebateseducation.co.uk
Enjoy ☺

1

"MISS, YOU LOOK SH*T": BOUNDARIES, NEGOTIATIONS AND CARE — FOR YOU

#INSULTOFTHEWEEK

Pupil: "Miss, you're unique."

Me: "Oh thanks."

Pupil: "No Miss, that is not a compliment."

IN THIS CHAPTER YOU WILL

- Learn how to hold our own boundaries for self-care in a culture that does not support it.
- Discover how holding these personal boundaries helps us support pupils with challenging behaviour.

INTRODUCTION

Yes. This a book about behaviour and we're starting with how you care for yourself.

Why? Because our young people with behavioural needs deserve the best.

These pupils have some of the greatest needs. They have some of the biggest challenges to being included in school, education and our society, because of their own experiences and attitudes, as well as the discrimination and prejudice that are stacked against them. Therefore, they present some of the most challenging behaviour to the adults around them, and that gets tricky sometimes. These pupils need the most capable educators supporting them. You have a responsibility to look after yourself, and I know that as teachers we're generally pretty rubbish at this, but that's no longer good enough. Whilst I advocate for an improved wellbeing focus in the education system's infrastructure, I also believe we have more power than we realise as educators on the ground. This chapter provides the first steps.

You have a responsibility to be ready to work with these vulnerable young people, to be as patient, as understanding and as human as you can be with them. So too right we begin with looking after ourselves. If we can't hold a boundary for ourselves to eat lunch every day, how can we hold a boundary for a pupil who we know is on the verge of self-destruction?

A COMMON SCENARIO

Please alter job roles in accordance with your situation.

> Lunchtime is forty minutes. After dealing with a behaviour incident, you've lost ten minutes. On your way to the canteen, your Head of Department grabs you to ask "can you just provide work for Deci who is still in hospital this week, recovering from her operation? It needs to go in the post this afternoon, as her laptop won't connect to the school's system, so I'll need it at the end of lunch." Your next lesson is the other side of the school, with the notoriously ill-behaved 9F2. You need to allow ten minutes to get there and check that the key for the cupboard that contains your equipment for the lesson is still in the drawer – if not, you need to find the caretaker.

So you're left with twenty minutes at best. Your options are:

- **Option A: Skip lunch** return to your classroom and find or create the work for Deci, spend an extra five minutes trying to find your HOD (who has gone into a meeting) and leave the requested work on her desk – wonder if her meeting will finish before the emergency post goes out.
- **Option B: Run back** to your classroom, pick up some worksheets to photocopy on your way back to the canteen, cross your fingers you can get served quickly, don't get caught in any incidents (or other requests) and buy the on-the-go-sandwich option – the same lunch you've had for the last three days.

- **Option C: Say no but offer an alternative** to have some work ready for tomorrow by breaktime.
- **Option D: Say an outright no** to your HOD.
- **Option E: What else can you think of?**

Before we investigate the implications of these options, I want to add a caveat: there are ideal world answers and there is reality. We can't always practice exactly what we would like to (because we are human). However, thinking through these options outside of the moment and preparing for them to reoccur, we can notice patterns and those moments where we kick ourselves for not doing or saying what we really wanted to – and thus we are more likely to make decisions we feel aligned with in the moment. The options:

OPTION A: SKIP LUNCH

FOOD

I have done this many times myself, especially when running my Amnesty International lunch club. If you needed proof that this affects your teaching, I would like to share this insightful observation from one of my pupils – a pupil classed as 'low ability' and unlikely to pass their exams:

Pupil: Miss you're being more snappy today, what's up?

Me: I'm fine, get on with your work.

Pupil: You're not usually this grumpy, have you had lunch?

Me: No, had a club.

Pupil: Eat your lunch Miss.

Me: We're not supposed to eat in front of you – rules.

Pupil: Please eat Miss.

Food is a basic need, and whilst I'm not going to go into a lecture about any type of diet or nutrition programme, I will advocate this:

Healthy diet (sleep pattern, exercise, lifestyle) = energy = patience, understanding and empathy – and a heightened ability to support pupils with challenging behaviour.

During my NQT year we had coaching sessions, the coach told us that one of the main 'takeaways that worked' for NQTs in all the coaching was to have a constant stash of high energy, healthy snacks in your teacher's desk. So simple, so helpful.

On a wider perspective, take some time to examine your food plan. You may have great intentions to get home with your veggie box and Ottolenghi meal every night. You manage it until Tuesday then you're put on a detention rota, there's an emergency meeting with some parents and reality is more beans on toast (with the mouldy bits picked out) most nights. Be realistic and get someone to help you – outside eyes are always good. You make two decent meals a week and then batch and freeze, one ready meal a week and a constant supply of healthy bars, bananas and dates (or whatever works for *you* to maintain a healthy body and mind) in your desk.

BOUNDARIES

I have been lucky enough to work with experienced Leadership Development Coach and founder of Inspiring Women Changemakers, Anju Handa who, in her clear guide on setting boundaries, advocates: "If you do not clearly demonstrate and communicate your boundaries, how can you expect others to respect them?" (Handa, 2020). She is completely right. Pupils pick up on how we act and how we respect ourselves – if they see you not holding boundaries with others, they will know (subconsciously) that they can push your boundaries later. You'll see many parallels with this later when we examine how to retain boundaries with pupils.

There is often a belief, especially when you start teaching, that you must do everything because everyone else is. MYTH BUSTER: this is not true, even if it appears like that from the outside with some people. Only *you* can decide where your boundaries are and only *you* can (lovingly) maintain them.

If you don't maintain your own boundaries then pupils, HOD, Governors, people who don't know how to queue properly, your children, your partner will all step over that boundary – sometimes without knowing that they are. This sets a pattern – they will experience this as the norm, and it will happen again:

- "Pleeeeeeeeaaasse Miss, can I sit next to my friend this lesson? Just once?" Say yes and they will ask you again next lesson. Your seating plan no longer exists.
- "You don't mind if we postpone your idea until next meeting, do you? Geoff needs to talk about the new visualisers." Say yes, and this will happen often with your ideas.
- "Please don't tell my Mum, she said I won't get the new iPhone for my birthday if school rang about my behaviour again.". Say yes, and not only will you be asked this again, but behaviour will deteriorate.

As a self-rule, hold your boundaries 99% of the time. The other 1% is that part that *is* for times that we're flexible, for ourselves, for an easier life and for others' ease. It's your judgement call, but be warned; if that percentage creeps past 1% of the time there will be consequences; will you still be able to reinforce the previous boundaries, or not?

OPTION B: RUN BACK

ENERGY

As an eternal optimist (or as my partner says – unrealistic) this is my favourite choice and usual downfall. Option B relies on luck and multitasking skills.

There are so many variables out of your control; if you *do* manage to pull it off that can be dangerous too – first you get a kick from succeeding, "I achieved everything despite the odds", then it may also come with external kudos, "I don't know how you manage it all", which the ego loves. The danger, however, is that the goalposts shift, sometimes without you noticing; this has then become your new norm. The result: you're not just doing this mammoth juggling act when your HOD asks a quick favour, but this becomes every lunchtime and break and afterschool.

One term I found myself simultaneously leading a Year 7 form of 35 *and* doing one-to-one interventions with my Year 11 GCSE pupils. This plate spinning can only be sustained for a limited length of time. Add an external factor – a cold, period pains, financial worries, family troubles or illness, an experience of racism, sexism, homophobia etc., and the whole thing goes pop.

If you are susceptible to Option B return to your own boundaries. Let's look at the physics again.

Imagine you are an energy bowl with a finite amount of energy dependant on the amount of sleep, food, physical and mental rest and exercise you get.

- How much energy do you have in your bowl right now?
- How much do you need for yourself?
- Do you have any spare?
- How many lunchtimes per week are you doing this juggling act?
- How many really? – A small tally by your desk can help if you are unsure.
- How many is realistically sustainable, how many would you have in an ideal world?

Note that some option Bers will not recognise their choices as a problem. Sometimes it's not – in the moment. We all work in different ways and have varying capacities for different things. But also look out for other areas in your life where the pressure is building. A classic is "keeping it all together" at school, but turning into a fire-breathing dragon at home, crying on the way to work regularly or losing the ability to really listen to people close to you.

OPTION C: SAY NO BUT OFFER AN ALTERNATIVE

There's an art to this, and it *can* be done successfully and in fact can be more positive in the long run. The art of holding boundaries, whilst negotiating, again, is a skill needed in bucket loads with pupils with challenging behaviour.

PART A: BOUNDARIES AGAIN

You must hold your own boundary and therefore self-worth with your HOD. Depending on their character or your relationship, this could be a quick non-thinking reflex or a monumental, heart wrenching undertaking.

Some doubts that might arise are: "can I really put my (pathetic sandwich with no butter because I ran out) lunch before a child's education? A child who is already ill? I need that pay rise next year and it's performance related, maybe this is a test of my performance? Everyone else skips lunch, I'm weak if I don't", and so on. These are all completely justified as thoughts, but they don't mean you need to automatically agree if you're not comfortable with doing so. There may also be differences in gender, race, age, status etc. that make you feel uncomfortable in saying no directly. Deborah Frances-White examines this power play between women and men, both when women are being asked for something and when consent is being assumed, "If someone takes without asking because they assume they're entitled, your no can come as a surprise to them and it can feel like a confrontation" (Frances-White, 2018: 211). If you feel holding your boundary would be interpreted as a confrontation, it is understandably harder to consider maintaining it. Frances-White then goes on to explain that sometimes saying no to someone within your community, a friend or someone you identify with can also be challenging, as "Their expectation of alliance is higher" (2018: 217). I have seen this play out in schools where, for example, a black pupil who is challenging a teacher's authority may revert to bringing up their similarities – the teacher is also black – to attempt to strengthen allegiance and avoid punishment. All these factors (and you will think of more) will be the underlying reasons why you find yourself agreeing to extra pressure or work that you know is not good for you, or your pupils. These are real feelings, thoughts and experiences and I'm not suggesting that you suppress them. Spending time thinking about these things outside of the context can be empowering, and I would like to invite you to tinker with the notion of alternative thoughts, and experiment with how that will play out next time. Explore the possibility that, if you eat your sandwich, and get twenty minutes to switch off, you'll be more able to handle 9F2 in period 5.

Remember:

Healthy diet (sleep pattern, exercise, lifestyle) = energy = patience, understanding and empathy – and a heightened ability to support pupils with challenging behaviour!

When Tyler starts telling you he "can't be arsed" with his coursework *again* after lunch, you'll have the patience and energy to take him aside, have a conversation with him, hold your boundaries and find a way forwards (unlike last week when you had to call pastoral after he set his book alight). Which brings me to the key message of this chapter:

You having time to refill your tank, physically, emotionally, energetically is the *best* thing you can do to help support pupils with challenging behaviour.

So once you've convinced yourself, or at least decided to entertain the idea, that your lunchtime is vital, you need to negotiate this with the HOD. Who may or may not agree with you.

PART B: NEGOTIATING

1. Understand: "Deci is still in hospital? I hope the operation went well. Yes, it's important we keep her learning going."
2. Set your boundary – no need to justify yourself: "I won't be able to create something now."

3. Offer an alternative: "However, I could adapt the sheets we're doing in a way she'd really enjoy and might be more suitable for the hospital environment. I could get this to you for tomorrow by first break."
4. Listen: Nine out of ten times the firm boundary and the alternative is enough for most managers to agree. If there are objections, repeat the process:

HOD: "But we really need it now."

You: "Yes, I can see the urgency." (Understand) "As I said, I'd be happy to get a suitable version of the work to you for tomorrow break time." (Maintaining set boundary) "If not, there is a copy of the key points we covered in the lesson on my desk, you can help yourself to this now and send it so she has something to at least read until I send her the work tomorrow." (Offering an alternative)

Note, you do *not* need to justify your (own, possibly unpaid!) time, do not offer that:

HOD: "But what are you doing now?" (Listen)

You: "Preparing for 9F2, I'm going to get on." (Maintaining boundary)

Preparing is a useful word – *we* know that preparing is you eating your lunch, getting a break and mentally preparing for 9F2. It does also encompass finding that key and setting up your equipment. You have been truthful and kept your boundary.

OPTION D: SAY AN OUTRIGHT NO

This option may be entirely appropriate. It could be the third time this week they've left it until the last minute for this type of request, you have already promised something similar or you feel it is not your task. Communicate clearly and neutrally. A succinct version of the previous conversation:

"Oh dear." (Understand) "That's not something I can help you with I'm off to prepare for 9F2." (Set boundary) "You could check the homework resources for something that's already ready?" (Offer alternative)

[space for response] (Listen)

"I can't help then, I must get off." (Maintain boundary)

OPTION E: WHAT ELSE CAN YOU THINK OF?

Have a think. Knowing your own weaknesses and strengths, are there other options? What do you see colleagues doing who are able to maintain boundaries more successfully? Think of a time you did successfully hold a boundary with someone, what did you do and how did it feel afterwards?

THE 1% SHIFT

It may be overwhelming (few of us are living the exact, self-care, boundaried, fun life we imagine *all* of the time), or you may not know where to start. The best way to find your first step, I have found, is inspired by Red School's work concerning the '1% shift', a method (explained in detail in the Action Box) that involves finding a small step you can take towards your overall aim. I am a graduate of the Menstruality Leadership Programme, in which I got to practice this approach in relationship to my menstruality – and for my self-care and work ethic in general. In their book *Wild Power,* Alexandra Pope and Sjanie Hugo Wurlitzer discuss "the power of small moves to make big changes [...] You may find yourself constantly sitting under the thumb of what you think you 'should' be doing, falling into 'idealised' thinking and abandoning the real possibilities before you" (Pope and Wurlitzer, 2017: 212). It's a sentence that resonates wholeheartedly with teaching and schools.

The 1% shift is a miraculous method. I know, I've tried and tested it and use it a lot. Within teaching it took me from feeling lost, stressed and out of control, to working with and on behalf of the pupils I enjoy working with the most, being the author of this book, being invited to do my TEDx talk, speak as an expert on teenage behaviour on BBC Radio 4 and spend much of my working life engaged and motivated. When I was working fulltime in a mainstream large comprehensive secondary, I knew that whilst it was 'good for my career' to get 'experience under my belt' that it wasn't working *for me*; which inevitably affected my teaching. As my Nana used to say, I couldn't see the wood for the trees. I didn't know what needed to change, but I promised myself I would start to explore the possibilities – 1%.

At the time I was mentoring a trainee teacher and one evening I went to the university to do top up training with them. I met with a co-ordinator of the PGCE course who had been there when I trained. She asked me how I was doing – I decided to tell the truth – the 1%! I felt like a fraud – *I* was there because *I* was the mentor, it was *me* who was supposed to be promoting the profession. However, I knew the balance in my life wasn't right. I shared honestly some of my experiences and frustrations about my role. The co-ordinator then set up fortnightly coaching sessions for me with one of the tutors – this was even free of charge because I was alumni. These happened *within school time* so as not to add any more hours to my day. It only lasted for around five sessions, but it was enough for me to work out that the current environment was not sustainable for me. With the support of the coach, I requested to go down to four days a week the following year – this was the magic. The extra day was exactly what I needed to give me clarity of my direction with education. Of course, there was a wage cut, however I accounted for most of that by taking on a Teaching and Learning Responsibility (TLR) within the school that enthused me – the Lead on Equality and Diversity – another important 1% shift that eventually led me on my path. The extra day a week gave me time to write, reflect and mostly just breathe. From there, it was a couple more terms until I decided that I needed to work on a freelance basis within schools and have time to write, train and speak on the inclusive education I am so passionate about creating.

My 1% approach (along with the Menstrual Cycle Awareness I was practising), led me to put myself first so that I can do the best for the pupils. Now I am teaching part time in a special school for SEMH pupils *and* I get to use my performance, communication and writing skills to advocate and train on behalf of these vulnerable pupils – who are so often voiceless. I could not have stepped here directly from the lost stress-head I was a few years ago – following my 1% crumbs was what did it.

I have re-purposed Red School's step-by-step explanation of the practice of the 1% shift for this chapter's Action Box.

FINLAND AND WELLBEING

At the start of 2019, I partook in a Finnish Education Research Trip observing, teaching and interviewing across five schools and with Local Authority equivalent policy makers (for more information see Further Reading). Beforehand, I had a list of research questions to ask the schools, staff and pupils. Because Finland is famous for its teacher trust and autonomy, that list included "How do you approach staff wellbeing?" It took me a week of feeling lost, but by the second school I realised I was asking the wrong questions. The schools I visited did not have specific staff wellbeing policies or added on tokenistic, well-meaning but ultimately useless events like 'Soup-vembers' (a well-meaning concept I once witnessed fall flat in a large British school, due to a lack of thought around logistics) because the infrastructure of Finnish education gives their teachers more flexibility in their timetables, more autonomy in the classroom, longer initial teacher training at a higher level (compulsory Master's degree for every teacher) and – possibly the magic bullet – no inspection body like Ofsted. Is everything therefore perfect in Finnish schools? Of course not, I saw a small number of stressed teachers and a rather spectacular canteen food fight during my visit. However, I also saw an overwhelming majority of teachers who were fully-fledged human beings; not teacher-robots. Every teacher I interviewed could list hobbies, leisure or extra learning that they actually did (not just listed on their CVs and dating profiles). When a teacher – or pupil – in Finland is not timetabled to be in lesson they are not expected to be on site. A teacher I stayed with for a week didn't have lessons until midday on a Monday that term. The time was hers – she could stay at home and plan, meet with parents and carers, walk the dog (in the metre thick snow), or have a lie in. When a school's timetable promotes that level of trust and individualised space for work-life balance, and therefore wellbeing, Soup-vembers are not necessary.

For those of us not teaching in Finland, or other countries with such approaches, we may not have this kind of flexibility and we may have to fight harder to maintain boundaries for our own self-care. It begins with knowing that taking the steps to maintain these vital practices for yourself and ultimately for your pupils is essential.

Interview

You're definitely not going to be at plus ten all the time. This is definitely not about pretending that everything is fine.

Frederika is a vivacious educator, speaker and consultant in Positive Psychology, specialising in Positive Education and Character Education. She has an MSc in Applied Positive Psychology and is currently studying for her Professional Doctorate in Education. She is the founder of "Educate to Flourish CIC", a not-for-profit organisation that supports children and provides them with tools to flourish in life. She is also the European Representative for IPPAed, the International Positive Psychology Association's Positive Education.

I have been lucky enough to collaborate with Frederika and witness her zest for life on many occasions – sometimes involving staying up until 2am enthusiastically putting the education system to right. Her personal circumstances have been full of challenges, not least in supporting her two daughters with ongoing serious medical issues, including open-heart surgery. Alongside this, however, she uses the tools of Positive Psychology to support her own wellbeing, and lucky for us she shares this in her work as an author, trainer and lecturer in Positive Education.

How can you teach and look after the wellbeing of children if you're not well yourself?

Beginning from the parent perspective, Frederika reminds us:

We entrust our most precious living being to teachers. They spend their entire days, most of their lives actually, with teachers. Why would we not want those teachers to be well? It's absolutely essential. The stats are horrific on teacher wellbeing; we need to do something. There's clearly stuff that needs to happen at a systemic level, but ultimately if you can't change the system and overhaul it, then you need to be able to do the stuff for yourself. I come from the perspective of Positive Psychology, and there are things that we can do. We live in an imperfect world, so we think: what can I do to protect myself to boost my resilience and look after my wellbeing as much as I can? I always think of it as using the tools as best you can to be the best you can be under the circumstances you find yourself in.

Frederika gives an oh-so-familiar example around behaviour from her years as a teacher, highlighting the teacher's common affliction of perfectionism and demonstrating the importance of accepting what you *can* do:

I felt like every lesson was a failure because I couldn't control the class, I couldn't control the behaviour. I spent most of the time being beetroot red

(Continued)

because I was about to explode. One of the big things to do in these circumstances is to focus on the little wins. There was one 15-year-old in my classes, he was very disruptive. He was one of the kids who was always one of the hard guys, 'no one messes with me' and I couldn't connect with him. Then one lesson, I don't know what had happened, he was just a delight. So at the end of the lesson I asked him to come over and he was looking like *what the ?!*&.* I just said to him, "I want you to know it was such a pleasure to teach you today. Whatever's gone on for you today, hold on to that because today you shone in this lesson." He just looked at me and said, "could you write that in my diary for my parents to read?" I said, "of course I will, I will do this for you every single lesson if that's what you want." It was just a tiny little breakthrough but 18 years later, that one moment – I can still remember that. Now if we can go through our day and instead of focusing on all the shit that piles upon us, we can focus on that one good thing that went really well that will help us.

Frederika also works with Character Strengths – 24 characteristics of our personality that affect how we think, feel and behave. Knowing where our strengths lie can be the key to us approaching challenging situations, by playing on these strengths and using them as a lens to fulfilment. Frederika gives an example: one of your strengths is curiosity, and you're having difficulty getting through your marking, how could you use this strength to re-frame the task? Maybe set up some enquiries – I wonder how many pupils spelt the key vocabulary wrong? Or I wonder how many Pupil Premium pupils understood the concept? There is more information and a survey to find out your own strengths at the VIA Institute on Character – and by completing it for yourself you also add to their data for the studies.

I asked Frederika what a key message would be to herself 18 years ago, struggling with behaviour in the classroom.

There is only one of you. In the extreme case, once you're gone, you're gone and if you let yourself be depleted and swallowed up by the job, by the stress and everything else then that's it. What else is there? However you show up, whatever you are able to do it has to be enough in that moment and you owe it to yourself to look after your wellbeing because it's much harder to get it back than to work on it.

Source: Interview with author, 2020

Action Box

Next lesson

Before your next lesson, set aside a minimum of five minutes of uninterrupted time.

Start by giving your imagination free rein and let yourself dream up what your teaching life and personal life could look like if you put yourself *first*. Get a large sheet of paper and coloured pens and dream big [...] how many hours are you working per week? How often would you cook? What would you eat? What sleep pattern would you have? How much time would you spend with your own children, family or friends? What type of school are you in? What type of pupils do you work with? How would you be treated by colleagues and pupils? What type of teacher are you? What kind of role do you have within the school? There are no limits. Don't censor yourself – dare yourself to use your imagination. (Keep this paper somewhere safe.)

Now ask yourself what 1% of that change would be. Let it be something really small, seemingly insignificant and imminently doable.

Make a small note of it where you will see it, on a Post-it, by your bed, on your phone.

Next week

Do your 1% shift.

Long term

Do the 1% shift regularly.

Schedule in another five minutes where you re-meet with your big dream. Get the paper out. See how the 1% shift has made a difference, consider shifting to 2% or finding another 1% in a different area. As Red School warn – it does get addictive.

What has any of this got to do with behaviour?

As educators, holding our own boundaries for self-care is necessary. Many of us do not work in a system that does this for us. It is different for everyone, spending time to find out what works for you specifically (at different times of the day, month or year) can pay dividends.

When you take radical responsibility for your own behaviour, you can make a bigger positive impact for others – your pupils.

Further reading

Setting Healthy Boundaries – Anju Handa

A useful cheat sheet outlining how to establish effective, authentic communication in the workplace that can be found at www.inspiring womenchangemakers.co.uk/cheat-sheets/ (accessed 26 March, 2021).

For Flourishing's Sake – Frederika Roberts

As well as outlining what Positive Education actually is, Frederika's latest book shares examples of the benefits of Positive Education, an international range of settings it can be used in, how it helps academic process and the practicalities of how staff are supported with it, how you might use it yourself in a school that does not support it and the cost implications. Published by Jessica Kingsley Publishers. Frederika also hosts the *For Flourishing's Sake* podcast at www.forflourishingssake.com/ (accessed March 26, 2021).

What on Earth makes Finnish Schools SO Good? – Adele Bates

A 3-part series of blog and vlog posts outlining the findings of my Finnish Education Research Trip. Topics covered include: inclusion, SEND, behaviour, Early Years, assessment, curriculum, staff structure, wages, parent and carer involvement:

https://adelebateseducation.co.uk/what-on-earth-makes-finnish-schools-so-good/ (accessed 26 March, 2021).

https://adelebateseducation.co.uk/finnish-education-part-2/ (accessed 14 April, 2021).

https://adelebateseducation.co.uk/finnish-education-balance-for-better-part-3/ (accessed on 14 April, 2021).

Wild Power – Alexandra Pope and Sjanie Hugo Wurlitzer (founders of Red School)

An absolute must for any menstruating person who wants to harness the power of their cycle, discover how to make school life work with the cycle and get rid of any inconveniences that it causes. It includes three 'maps' to guide you through the energies, tasks and challenges presented as you journey through each cycle. A well-thumbed copy of this sits on my bedside table at all times. Published by Hay House with accompanying podcast Wild Power Series.

2

"MISS, THERE'S NO WAY I'M COMING TO YOUR CLASS": SAFETY FIRST (LEARNING SECOND)

#INSULTOFTHEWEEK

Collecting a student from their taxi:

Student: "Miss, why are you collecting me today?"
Me: "Because it's my turn, anything wrong with me collecting you?"
Student: "Your face."

> **IN THIS CHAPTER YOU WILL**
>
> - Understand that safety is different for each of us, and how safety affects learning potential for our pupils.
> - Learn how to create safety for your pupils by setting up and maintaining boundaries and routines.
> - Get an introduction to trauma informed practice.

INTRODUCTION

Safety first looks simple and obvious, but without it, your lesson, workshop or assembly will not work. As this chapter's #InsultOfTheWeek suggests, for some pupils a different face can be enough to provoke feelings of unsafety at school. It took me 45 minutes to persuade this Autistic pupil to leave the taxi and walk the 20 metres into school since her key worker was away – I had the wrong face.

I often work in educational settings with students who have experienced the kind of trauma that's difficult to talk about, sometimes at a very early age. The fear they have around being in a room alone with an adult, being in a room with a closed door, being part of a large crowd, being requested to do something by an adult they don't know – these situations can trigger devastating memories that they don't have the capacity to understand and your attempt to just 'get them to learn one quote' will come to nothing. Rachel W's interview at the end of this chapter gives us a very personal insight into how real the threat to safety can be for our pupils who have experienced trauma, abuse or neglect.

Sometimes this step is barely noticeable – you walk into a high ability Year 8 class who are thirsty for knowledge and you teach them the subject you're passionate about. They feel safe with the usual teacher-student setup; they know that they must be quiet(ish) when you stand at the front, they understand that they must put their hand up to ask a question, and that in general they must sit on the seat and at the desk. Whether this is true respect towards you, their peers and education itself or learnt compliance is another thing to discuss, but at this point the pupils are able to self-regulate enough (on the main unconsciously) so you are able to get straight to the teaching and learning – blissful (if you like that kind of thing).

Sometimes however, this step can take weeks, terms, years to establish. Sometimes it eludes us completely, depending on the needs of the students. You're the fourth short term supply teacher a class has had this term. They are completely lost on the curriculum and have developed a deep distrust for any adult stood in front of them. They don't believe that you'll stay either, so why bother listening or working? They did this assessment last term, why should they do it again just because the last teacher unexpectedly left one Friday, took the assessments and never returned?

A colleague of mine once shared a challenging experience: in his training years he was asked to work alone with a female, foreign pupil on her English Literacy skills as she was learning English as an Additional Language (EAL). As a keen trainee, he went about trying the new strategies for EAL literacy that he had been taught himself the week before. After a short time, he noticed that the pupil was very quiet, gave monosyllabic answers and seemed quite scared. Whatever he tried, failed to engage her in the work and with little experience he didn't know what to do about it. It wasn't until *after* the session that his Mentor disclosed to him that this girl had been raped by a man in the country she had just fled.

Unless we feel safe and included, we cannot learn.

Literacy skills (even if they could unlock your very experience of the new country you're in), will come second if you feel you are in potential danger. My colleagues who are pioneering education work with refugees in camps know this first step all too well. You can't take it for granted that once you have created this safe environment that it will remain a constant either.

A trans student I had supported through their early months of transitioning had built up huge confidence in my class. Going from a shy girl who would not even read aloud, he was now a confident young man who took on the role of Orsino in our class reading of Twelfth Night. In just a few weeks, alongside coming out to his friends, me (as the first adult – an honour) and then his parents, he had changed his name and negotiated most of the tricky conversations with peers, teachers and school about why he could be called by that name, despite his official documents still being in his birth name for now. Interestingly, I had noticed that he was now able to use apostrophes correctly – a skill that had eluded him for nearly two years previously, no matter what I had tried. He was able to be himself, he felt safe and therefore he had space within himself for new learning – like apostrophes.

Then one day a girl from another class was moved to mine due to 'bad behaviour'. The trans student became a different person. He could only sit at the side of the classroom, near the door. He could no longer speak in front of the class and asked to leave regularly. I discovered that he had had a negative experience with this new pupil, when he first started transitioning. I don't believe my student took in any of Act 3, Act 4 or possibly any of the rest of the play – it took another six weeks until I was able to recreate the safe environment for him. Despite having built such a positive, safe relationship with my trans student, the new threat trumped the learning.

The re-engagement process was laborious; initially finding out what the issue was, discreetly holding firm boundaries with the new girl – that did not highlight the trans student's part in it. The least useful thing for me to do in this instance would be to refer to that – I would have given her an opening for out of class bullying. Instead, I had to be vigilant about *any* forms of her behaviour that were not in our class' unofficial respect and behaviour agreements. Essentially, I had to win this new girl around to this class' culture: we accept people of all gender identities in this class, for us it is not an issue. At the same time I had to allow the new girl to have her own space to feel safe and welcomed. I was not expecting her to conform at the detriment of her own identity or values, but work out what would be and not be appropriate behaviourally in her new class. I also have to admit that throughout this

I was actually quite annoyed that the new girl's entrance had slowed down the progress and learning of the trans student, and taken a lot of my energy away from the class as a whole – the other 33 pupils. But, I know that if one person doesn't feel safe it quickly spreads. The trans student had many good friends in the class, I'm sure it would make great breaktime gossip to talk about how *awful* it had become in English since *new girl* had arrived – at the possible risk of then having new girl become the victim herself. My job as the classroom teacher is to create a safe space and inclusive culture for *all* my pupils with *all* of their differences.

Unless we feel safe and included, we cannot learn.

So how do we do it? How can we account for all the different people sat in front of us, and what may or may not make them feel safe?

ROUTINES AND CONSISTENCY

I am yet to find something written about behaviour management in the classroom that does not address this issue. As humans, routines and consistency make us feel safe and comfortable. We know that ourselves from our own experiences:

- Ran out of coffee and didn't get your usual morning cup? – you notice it.
- Forgot your phone? – you notice it.
- You didn't do your usual walk with the dog before work? – you notice it.
- Your usual train is cancelled and you have to take a replacement bus? – you notice it.
- The supply teacher is drinking from *your* mug in the staffroom? – Grrrrr.

It is the same for our pupils, and more so. The teenage years are a time to experiment with identity, take risks and push boundaries. At this stage, their brains are less developed in the pre-frontal cortex, the part of the brain that is responsible for thought, analysis and rationality (read more in Chapter 5). Whilst we can understand the biology behind the perceptions of safety, we need to take this one step further. We need to consciously build in that safety in order to help the pupils regulate when they are unable to do so themselves.

There is a myth that if you approach behaviour from the idea that relationships come first, that connection needs to precede correction or that all behaviour is communication, then you are somehow 'fluffy' and wouldn't use routines or boundaries. This is false. Humans create routines and boundaries in our everyday lives and society to create safety and order; my guess would be that we created this culture as we saw it mirrored in our surroundings naturally – we have seasons, day and night, menstrual cycles, different stages of growth – and so this shape is naturally followed in our schools. We have lesson times, playtimes, lunchtimes. We have timetables and rules that (if we're lucky) are for the safety and order of all within the school community. These are good for behaviour; for *everyone's* behaviour. What you discuss in the staffroom or department office might not land so well with the pupils in your classroom; as a Secondary English teacher I don't have to worry too much whether my pupils can use a drill (thank goodness), and my pupils know that throwing a ball in my class will have very different consequences to doing so in their PE lessons – and we all know that the rules at a Christmas or Wintertime staff party are very different to Monday morning back in school.

THE THREE NON-NEGOTIABLES

On a classroom level, I stick by the three non-negotiables. These are not hard-and-fast rules, they are not something that I need to enforce on my colleagues, but they are a part of my own classroom practice, and they can be anything, the action itself is almost irrelevant. For example, one of mine might be that there is no talking during the register (unless you're answering, there's always one smarty pants). This makes sense, as the register is vital for safeguarding, but it also sets the tone for my lessons by providing a moment of calm in their usual busy, overstimulated days and provides a clean slate to the lesson. I explicitly share the benefits of the expectation, communicating that this could be of practical benefit to all of us, not just something to give me power and compliance. With a new class, or a class that has gone awry, this may take a surprisingly long time and at times seem hopeless, creating the temptation to not bother sticking to it yourself, *but don't*. What establishing this routine does is create the culture and expectations in your classroom. It breaks down something like this:

- You communicate clearly one of the behavioural expectations in your classroom, along with the benefits you understand.
- You allow room for questions and objections. Be prepared to take on adaptations, pupils know things you don't about how the classroom runs.
- You explain any consequences that may occur if the expectations are not followed. This is not necessarily a punishment, but could also be a safety consequence or an explanation of how that might affect them or others, depending on the action.
- You role model or 'rehearse' the behaviour as appropriate.
- You put the practice into action.
- You allow time for everyone to get used to it.
- Some pupils may forget, find it difficult, need reminders.
- You remind them of the expectation and the consequences calmly, knowing that this is not a personal dig at your authority, but an incubation period of a new expectation.
- If some pupils have difficulty you communicate with them individually and away from the others, firstly to find out if there is a barrier stopping them from managing the expectation, helping them with that if necessary, and finding a way that they can achieve it. For example, a pupil with ADHD may not be able to sit still and quiet for as long as it takes to get through the register sometimes, there may be underlining anxiety issues around silence without distraction that comes out as disruptive behaviour – they need to fiddle with something, and so you provide them with that, and re-instate the expectation and consequence.

- If a punishment is attached to your consequences, then this must be followed up *every* time.
- Eventually the new routine will be set, pupils will see the benefits of participating. If they don't, that is a suggestion that either the expectation is not appropriate for this set of pupils, or there are further barriers to achieving it that you must investigate. For example, I worked in a school with profoundly disabled teenagers, some of whom made involuntary noises – silent register taking would not be appropriate for this setting. In another instance, I watched a mentee's class struggle with this action at certain times of day, so instead we put in a physical, stretching aspect to the register which helped the pupils to regulate themselves ready for learning, much less time was taken telling pupils off – and the register still got taken.
- I have found that once three non-negotiables are in place in this way, it makes other requests far more manageable, and you won't have to go through this process in as much detail every time. This is because *trust* and *safety* have been established.
- This process must also sit alongside your focus on building (or re-building) positive relationships with the pupils. I am far more likely to follow the routines and boundaries of someone I know who cares about me, sees me and I know has my best interests at heart.

WHEN RULES GO WRONG

I purposely think of my non-negotiables not as rules because they are not one-hundred-percent-set-in-stone. Rules that aspire to be like that, sometimes called 'zero tolerance', set themselves up for a fall because there are always exceptions that will need to be made – if the fire alarm goes, I am not going to insist on zero tolerance towards untucked shirts. Sticking with the register example, if I approach it as a 'zero tolerance rule' that there must be silence during the register then what do I do the day that Sarah gets a nosebleed and asks Svobodka for a tissue? I deal with the bleeding nose. I am proud that my pupils can help each other out. Punishing Sarah for 'breaking the silence rule' would clearly be non-sensical in this situation. Context is everything, compassion and kindness are required. We hold the routines and boundaries 99% of the time – so that when we do allow flexibility within them, it makes sense. That 1% allows us to respond to what's actually happening in front of us with the human beings we are responsible for. As many-years-ex Headteacher, author and teacher trainer David Gumbrell described to me recently, this is 'live teaching.'

Another example: Aadrij has not been to school for three weeks, he has severe mental health problems and the adults at home are struggling to cope with his extreme and sometimes violent mood swings. One day he manages to come to your class – but he is wearing trainers. The school has a strict no-trainers-policy on uniform. What do you do? Is this really the moment to issue a punishment, the first moment you've seen him in three weeks? But then if you don't, what message does that send to the rest of the pupils about the rule? Aadrij needs to feel safe and welcomed in your classroom, if not, it will be another three weeks until you see him again – and ultimately, it's his learning progress that suffers. Children have a huge sense of injustice and unfairness, rightly so, however they are also a lot more accommodating and resilient than most adults – they haven't spent as long set in their ways. With the pupil who complains that Sarah spoke during the register or that Aadrij is wearing trainers I have a conversation, I create a learning moment out of it about context and compassion. I can still talk to Aadrij at the end of the day – expressing how pleased I am to see him, highlighting his achievements and hopes for tomorrow, then I can mention his footwear, find out if he has rule-fitting shoes, and if not, find out how school could help him get them.

The other way that rules go wrong is when they create unquestioning compliance.

A silent class that's writing furiously *could* be learning and achieving lots. They could also be doodling and lost, scared to break the rule and express their need for help. Conscientious pupils often fall into this trap; they believe the rules are of higher importance than the learning, so afraid are they to break them, they sacrifice their own progress.

TRAUMA INFORMED PRACTICE

For some pupils, the word 'safety' may sound a little over dramatic, and for the fortunate ones, it may not be a conscious thing they have to think about. In that case, you can replace the word 'safety' with the idea of 'ideal learning or working environment.' As I write this, I feel safe and secure, but my chair is awful for my posture and I need the loo; I can still do my work but imagine how much easier I could access my work or my learning if I had the ideal environment (*takes a loo break*).

For others, safety is an absolutely necessary consideration – and it will look different for each person. Physical safety may be a more overt factor, but emotional safety can be hidden, and the pupil may not necessarily be able to communicate their needs; it might show as disruptive behaviour instead.

In Chapter 4 Frédérique Lambrakis-Haddad shares the vital detective process we partake in when working with vulnerable pupils. In this section, I will introduce the concept of trauma, how it can affect a pupil's behaviour and learning, and what we can do about it.

> You may think of trauma as an earthquake, terrorism or an assault. It is all these things, but it is also any event, or series of events, that overwhelms a person's capacity to cope with a long-lasting impact on that person. (Lambrakis-Haddad, 2020)

If the pupils you teach have experienced trauma, in any form, this will have had an impact on them and how they are able to be and interact with others. This is the part that is most relevant to us as educators. Trauma informed practice is being aware of this and taking measures to ensure that pupils are not re-traumatised in their learning environment. For many of us the effects of COVID-19 and a global pandemic have highlighted how important this awareness of trauma impact is. As Souers and Hall (2016) advise, it is not that we need to know the whole story of

each pupil, in fact that might lead to us getting caught up in that rather than helping in the present,

> we do, however, see the story's lingering effects [...] it is much more helpful
> for me to monitor the *effect* of the event on each individual, not to preoccupy
> myself with the details of the event itself [...] moreover, we can begin to see
> students as more than their story. (2016: 16)

A term often referred to when discussing trauma is ACEs – Adverse Childhood
Experiences – initially collated in the 1990s as a list of eight by Dr Anda and
Dr Felitti (Souers and Hall, 2016) in their study of 17,000 adults about the types of
situations that would cause a traumatic impact for a person:

- Substance abuse in the home
- Parent separation or divorce
- Mental illness in the home
- Witnessing domestic violence
- Suicidal household member
- Death of a parent or loved one
- Parental incarceration
- Experience of abuse (psychological, physical, emotional) or neglect (emotional, physical)

Nowadays, we also recognise the adverse effects of discrimination and oppression on minority groups that can lead to systemic adversity, prejudice, violence,
murder and genocide. With their list, they gave a value of one to each ACE. They
found the higher the 'score' a person had, the more likely they were to experience
health difficulties such as hepatitis, depression, immunity, lung cancer and heart
disease; and that 67% of the population had at least one ACE, and 1/8 had four or
more ACEs (Souers, and Hall, 2016). Dr Nadine Burke Harris' fantastic TED talk
explains this clearly:

> We now understand, better than we ever have before, how early exposure to
> adversity affects the developing brains and bodies of children...there are real
> neurologic reasons why folks exposed to high doses of adversity are more likely
> to engage in high risk behaviour [...] and even if you don't engage in high risk
> behaviour, you're still more likely to develop heart disease or cancer. (Burke
> Harris, 2014: 7.02 and 7.45)

Interestingly for schools, Dr Burke Harris found that many children diagnosed with
ADHD did not have that condition but had experienced several ACEs: what our
pupils have been through or are going through outside of the classroom affects their
behaviour inside the classroom through no fault of their own.

The disruptive behaviour is the pupils' own (conscious or unconscious) way of
dealing with the intensity of emotions they are experiencing, and as Souers and Hall
suggest, it is our place to not get swept up in this 'tornado':

the motivation is often clear, the disruption takes the focus away from the self and the discomfort of the current circumstance [...] Not only do we want to help the student see how his (sic) body is responding and how he (sic) can head off his (sic) own tornado, but we must also maintain our own sense of control. (2016: 57)

This refers to the control we have over ourselves in the classroom.

Educational Psychologist Dr Chris Moore outlines practical ways that we can make our classrooms trauma informed, and provide a safe base for learning. He refers to many themes covered in this book:

- **Belonging** – welcoming pupils into the learning environment in a way that makes them feel trusted and safe (see Chapter 7).
- **Predictability** – routines, boundaries, clear communication of activities and unforeseen changes.
- **Organisation** – a clear, low-sensory level environment can reduce stress.
- **Regulation** – consistent use of vocabulary, role modelling of expressing emotions and helping regulate more challenging ones (see Chapter 5).
- **Differentiation** – accounting for the challenges some young people face while concentrating on tasks (see Chapter 4).
- **Relationship** – nurturing trusting relationships are the foundation of safety (see Chapter 3).

Dr Moore has many articles and practical resources on his website, see Further Reading at the end of this chapter. To conclude this section, I refer once again to Souers and Hall who provide a clear approach to supporting some of our most vulnerable pupils:

By adopting a strength-based approach, you will see the wonder beneath the chaos. By seeking solutions rather than dwelling on problems, you will discover the path to success in partnership with each student. By understanding the 'why' behind behaviours, you will foster a safe and secure environment in which 'it's OK to be not-OK.' And by nurturing and holding high expectations for your students, you will build relationships that enable students to grow, thrive and learn at high levels. (Souers and Hall, 2016: 2)

Interview

Who cares about what ten times ten is, when that pupil has just been abused, lost his whole family and is living in a strange place in a whole new county? Who cares what ten times ten is? He needs to know that he will be safe again.

(Continued)

Rachel is a Canine Assisted Therapist, with over 20 years' experience working with pupils with SEMH. She has been a supervising learning support manager and intervention training behaviour specialist for local authorities all over the country, managing challenging behaviour for the staff and children in a residential children's home with a therapeutic base. Rachel W has been a Foster Mamma for teens and was a child in care herself, so has first-hand experience of abuse – whilst trying to access an education as a child and teen. I have had the honour of working alongside Rachel for three years in a SEMH school. She has taught me endless amounts about the children I work with, how best to support them and how to look after myself in the process. She is a true expert in this field.

In terms of safety in education, Rachel begins with emotional safety:

the emotional has a knock-on effect on the physical, more than we give it credit for, so if we've got that feeling of security and safety, the body can relax; when the body relaxes, we can then go into learning. In the education system I've learned and worked in, it's mostly education first, but then the learning's not going on.

In order to create safety, Rachel stipulates that it's about taking time and space to learn a child's patterns of behaviour. She exemplifies this with a story of one of the pupils at the therapeutic-based care home she worked:

There was one kid who utterly broke my heart – when he came in without his tie, we knew it would be a bad day. We knew the patterns of behaviour after learning them, which then gave us strategies to be able to help him to be able to deal with it. So then if he did come into school without a tie, we'd send him straight home, knowing that until he came into school with his tie that he wouldn't be capable of learning and he would cause so much disruption. We used to have to hold (restrain) him a lot, because of the effects of him still experiencing abuse at home. As much as we knew what was happening, we had to evidence it for anything to get done. So we'd send him home, he'd would put his tie on and come back in – now we would know we wouldn't have to restrain him for three to four hours at a time. The restraining – the physical, therapeutic management, maintained the physical safety, but the emotional safety is all about learning a kid's patterns of behaviours, what works, what doesn't and tailoring everything to what they need.

The key to getting this right, Rachel explains, is being aware of *every* behaviour.

No behaviour goes unnoticed, the positive and the negative. It begins with trial and error, and giving them the time to be themselves […] Pupils with SEMH need more attention because they've been through more.

I remember saying to a teacher: "If you let me take him out of class for ten minutes, you will get forty minutes of work from him." She would retort "but you're rewarding bad behaviour" "No," I explained, "I'm trying to get him into the right frame of mind to learn." We'd go for a drive around the block with music blasting, dancing away – getting the physical side in place, he knew I enjoyed spending time with him. Then we'd go back into class and he would sit and he would learn.

Another key to this work is relationships:

> The kids need to know that *we* give a shit. In fostering, as a Foster Mamma you bring in this secure base, it's about nurturing. Then when you get them almost able to accept the nurture, which most of them can't to start with, they see that you care and you're teaching them how to care. We need to explicitly teach what care is. I fostered an 11-year-old boy who had never had a story read to him – and I didn't think to do it until a friend suggested it, because I had never had a story read to me.
>
> We need to create this safety by role modelling – this has a massive part to play in a relationship. By the way that we look, the way we hold our bodies, the way that we talk; if we don't role model what safety is, whether that's putting in a boundary, sticking to a boundary or showing care, if we show that the kids will feel that, even if they don't recognise it. If they hear someone say "don't be so stupid", "don't be so silly" or "get a grip", "why don't you just grow up?" even if they've heard it before, they will instinctively know that this is not a safe adult, even if they don't know why – they will feel themselves being put down.
>
> Bring in the empathy first, bring in that feeling of security and need – you want them to be there and to thrive.

Finally, I asked Rachel to talk us through a scenario of supporting a pupil in physical and emotional danger in a classroom, in the heightened moment itself:

> First, ask them to stop. Ask them what's wrong. When a kid is right up there, they sometimes don't know that they *can* stop. They need an out, but their survival strategies, from whatever they've come from or whatever physiological condition is going on, puts them in that place. So if they're not shown how to behave, then they're going to presume what they're doing is OK.
>
> I know what it's like to be a kid who has suffered trauma and who can't hear in a particular situation what sum they want me to do because I'm too busy flashbacking over what happened the night before. Knowing what that's like and seeing the frustration of the teacher gives me an insight. What I, or any person who has suffered, does not need is sympathy, but an empathetic approach. I have seen kids broken by the system because they weren't given enough time, because they weren't seen for who they are, those kids become phobic of school.
>
> What worries me is that there's no time for the child, that it's all about the statistics, the exams, the Ofsted; but the most important thing is the kid and our impact on the kid. The kids are still not being heard, the mistakes are still being made and there's less and less time for the individual.

Source: Interview with author, 2020

Action Box

Next lesson

Ask the pupils to move to the space in the room they feel most comfortable. I use this with pupils and trainings with adults often – it demonstrates where people feel safe. If appropriate ask them the reasons for their choices.

Can you adapt your seating plan to accommodate this more? Especially pupils who have expressed feeling better by the door/window for example.

Next week

Choose 2–3 pupils who have particularly challenging behaviour for you. Find out three things about their home lives, for example who they live with, where they lived before, where they live, who they share a room with, which environments do they enjoy and struggle with and so on. If possible, arrange a home visit.

Long term

Look at your long term planning. Consider how the content and execution can be differentiated to make your most vulnerable pupils feel safe in your classroom and with the learning, e.g. if a pupil has difficulty with group work, how can you support this over a term to increase their confidence? Find out if any topics you are studying might be triggering for a child and differentiate accordingly. You may need to engage in additional research or CPD on new topics.

What has any of this got to do with behaviour?

When your pupils do not feel safe, it will affect their behaviour. They may not be able to precisely articulate the issue, and each pupil's feeling of safety will look different. It is our jobs as educators to investigate how we can make an optimum environment for our pupils to learn. For some, it will simply be pulling the blinds down, for others it may mean a long-term investment in building secure relationships with them – in a way no adult has ever done. Either way, before a pupil feels safe, they will be unable to learn, and you will be more likely to spend your time dealing with behaviour instead of teaching.

Further reading

How Childhood Trauma Affects Health Across a Lifetime – Dr Nadine Burke Harris
   A hard hitting and informative TED talk by paediatrician Dr Nadine Burke Harris, highlighting the direct effects of ACEs on the development of a young brain and the consequential health complications that affect the young person's behaviour, ability to learn and live. Available at www.ted.com/talks/nadine_burke_harris_how_childhood_trauma_affects_health_across_a_lifetime#t-303342 (accessed March 26, 2021).

Fostering Resilient Learners: Strategies for Creating a Trauma-Sensitive Classroom – Kristin Souers with Pete Hall (2016)
   A useful book for teachers and schools, grounded in research that clearly explains trauma informed practice in a school setting, and what educators can do to support their pupils.

Resilience: The Biology of Stress and Science of Hope – James Redford and Karen Pritzer
   A documentary film that explores the science of ACEs and the dangerous biological syndrome that can be caused by the toxic stress associated with them. It introduces the movement to treat and prevent toxic stress. https://kpjrfilms.co/resilience/ (accessed March 26, 2021).

EdPsychInsight – Dr Chris Moore
   Useful resources for educators, Dr Chris Moore's website and blog shares approaches to help young people with additional needs and the adults who work with them. www.epinsight.com (accessed March 26, 2021).

3

"MISS, YOU ARE NOT MY MUM": BUILDING RELATIONSHIPS

#INSULTOFTHEWEEK

Pupil: "Miss, what does patronising mean?"

Me: "When you talk down to someone as if they're younger or inferior to you in a bad way."

Pupil: "Oh, you mean like you did in our first ever lesson together?"

IN THIS CHAPTER YOU WILL

- Learn why building positive relationships is the way to improve behaviour in the classroom.
- Understand how to build positive relationships with pupils, in order to help them engage in learning.

INTRODUCTION

How we interact with children and build relationships with them affects their behaviour.

In the 1970s, Dr Ed Tronick developed The Still Face experiment (see Further Reading for links to watch a short video). The experiment gives us an understanding of how the emotional development of a child is dependent upon the type of interactions they receive from their primary adults at an early age. If a lack of interaction occurs often, it can negatively affect how the child interacts with others, how much they can trust others and how they get on in society.

Taking this into the classroom, the way we interact with our pupils will directly affect their behaviour. A smile at the door, a welcome to the classroom sets up a positive interaction from which to build. In contrast, "take your coat off, I told you that last week" accompanied by a frown, sets a negative tone to the lesson, and later the relationship. Unlike the Still Face experiment, you are less likely to be the child's primary adult, and there will already be patterns in place that will reflect how they have been treated by adults up to this point. Take this to heart – most often a pupil's negative response or refusal to engage with you in a relationship has very little to do with *you* (more on this in Chapter 6). Once you know this, and understand the child better, as the adult *you* can be the one to instigate and sustain a positive relationship – even when a pupil does not have the tools or previous experiences to do so.

CONNECTION BEFORE CORRECTION

With pupils with additional behavioural needs, we cannot take for granted that they will have learnt an unquestioning respect, or feelings of safety, towards new adults. In special SEMH schools where I work, this lesson is brought to me tenfold; when a young person cannot assume that a new adult is safe due to significant trauma, instigated sometimes by a close adult, they are on alert. They very consciously construct the first impression you have of them. There is an element of performance, which acts as a defence mechanism – the only way the child has learnt to keep themselves safe.

- The behaviour = F*** off (thrown chairs, aggression, smirks or *The Blank*).
- In contrast, the message = You're a new adult. I cannot trust you. Some adults do bad things to me. It's safer to not let you close.

Hence why, as Clinical Psychologist Kim S. Golding (2015) argues, "Connection before Correction" is a vital strategy for working with pupils with challenging behaviour. Transferring this into an educational setting, it is clear that the relationship that we build with the young person is the *first step* to improving their behaviour – and yet often this can go against our instinct as an adult attempting to exert boundaries and discipline within a classroom.

Golding explains that if a child has had a secure attachment (more about this in Chapter 4) with a primary caregiver(s) at an early age, they have learnt that they are loved unconditionally – no matter if sometimes there are seemingly negative actions from the caregiver – being shouted at or boundaries being put in place. In contrast, when a child does not have a secure attachment with the caregiver, it plays out differently; the child feels that negativity towards them is about *themselves* rather than the *actions*. The child has learnt that they are shameful. The core belief becomes 'I am shameful or bad'. If this pattern is repeated, it ingrains the belief further and transfers to other scenarios. "Children who mistrust therefore learn to resist authority and to oppose parental influence... They trust in themselves rather than others. These children develop controlling behaviours as they try to take charge of their own safety. It feels safer to be in charge than to be influenced by another" (Golding, 2015: 3).

Back in the classroom, when the teacher shouts at the child, or by this time young person, to be quiet or take their hat off, the same emotions are triggered; an adult is expressing negative behaviour towards them, they cannot trust that this adult has their best interests at heart, so they have to control the situation themselves – "f*** off, Sir", or head on the table. All of which re-affirms the core belief – I am shameful or bad.

Evidentially, this is not a useful frame of mind from which to begin formal learning.

To *only* enforce discipline and punishment at this stage does little to change the learnt pattern. The shame will increase and the disengagement with learning increases too. Instead, Golding (2015) advises that we develop boundaries and discipline *alongside* building a positive, trusting relationship. Given some children's experiences, this will take longer for them than for pupils who have had secure attachments in their early years.

MEDIA AND WIDER SOCIETY'S PERCEPTIONS

Our media and society at large do little to help this situation. Teenagers or 'yooves' are often depicted as 'hoodied hooligans', too loud, too sweary, inconsiderate, and so on. Open any (digital) newspaper, and the negative stories about teenagers far outweigh the positive. This is a misrepresentation – "Teenager does their homework on time, helps parents stack the dishwasher and always says hello to 86-year-old Doris at the bus stop" does not make the headlines. In addition, in the UK teenagers can *legally* be discriminated against unlike any other group.

We have signs in shops: 'Only two teenagers allowed at one time'. Replace 'teenagers' with any other minority group, and there would, quite rightly, be complaints in line with the Equality 2010 Act. Jay Griffiths' (2014) highly insightful book *Kith* examines the 'Childscape' that is now available for our young people – the environment and places they are able to feel safe, explore and just be children – has changed significantly in the West in the past few decades. Her investigation paints a worrying picture about the kind of overt and subliminal messages our young people are receiving, and how this informs how society relates to them:

> Children are discriminated against on public transport and by public services: they are often refused entry to libraries, leisure centres, museums and art galleries, so the commons of public place is cornered off to them [...] while dispersal orders give the police power to clear two or more kids who have committed no crime whatsoever. (Griffiths, 2014: xx)

When we know we are not welcome or safe, we become protective of ourselves, unlikely to open and form relationships – this is human nature.

Again, this is not a useful frame of mind from which to begin formal learning.

SO WHAT CAN WE ACTUALLY DO?

Firstly, educators, whilst often described as *in loco parentis* (in place of a parent), very rarely are a pupils' parent. In addition, there will most likely be several other pupils in the class, and in mainstream comprehensive teaching there is very little time for one-to-one dedicated relationship building. As such, we must find ways that we can build this into the normal lessons alongside compulsory curriculums.

FIRST IMPRESSIONS

As this chapter's #InsultOfTheWeek demonstrates, first impressions count, and clearly I still need to work on the Children's TV presenter style that can slip out when I'm nervous and meeting 30+ Year 10s whom I will be teaching for the next two years. Whilst you *can* claw back bumpy starts, if you intentionally set out well it can help no end in building positive relationships with your pupils that will make learning a lot easier.

Your job is to ensure there *is* a welcome – *however* the young person presents to you initially. If the pupil or class have a reputation for being 'bad', then they will expect to be treated that way, and will fulfil the prophecy. If we don't welcome them, we cannot be surprised if they react with negative behaviour – smile, be interested, welcome them into your learning space. They may not know at first how to *receive* a positive welcome; some, unfortunately, will not have received it often – but do it and keep doing. I am a fan of Paul Dix's (@PaulDixTweets) #ShakeyHandGang movement if it feels comfortable for you – stand on the threshold of your classroom and shake hands (fist pump, dance, whatever works in your context) with each pupil *every* time they enter – find what the virtual learning equivalent is for you. See what happens after two weeks.

The final bit to this is forgiveness – and *you* are the adult, so yes, it's *your* job to role model this first. If the pupils are not pleasant back to you the first – or first hundred – times, forgive them, welcome them again next lesson.

A pupil may start out with you in a challenging way – it's a test. Every time you meet them anew be welcoming, be warm, be kind.

FIRST IMPRESSIONS AND IDENTITY

A note that different pupils will react to different adults in different ways (and you to them) depending on how you look – your gender identity, your skin colour, your age, your accent, your weight, your physical ability, your energy and so on will garner various responses – even before you have said anything. When it comes to behaviour this can work both for and against us. As a white, cis, female teacher, often perceived to be 'young', 'bubbly' and 'energetic', pupils and colleagues expect certain things from me before they know me; it is usually that I would be offended by swear words, too fragile to deal with aggression and might need help from a (usually male) member of staff to deal with behaviour. When this impression is formed by colleagues it is frustrating, undermining and often unhelpful. When it comes to the pupils it can often work on my side – they don't *expect* me to be able to hold firm boundaries, not be phased by being told I'm a "gay bisexual c***" and still keep turning up, caring for them and helping them learn.

I believe this discussion of identity and managing behaviour is an important conversation. For now, in relation to building relationships, it is useful to know how you *may* be perceived by pupils and how you can work with that when forming relationships. The old adage 'be yourself' is key here. Any sniff of inauthenticity the pupils will know and lose respect for you – and if they're the type of pupils I work with, they will not be afraid to tell you in four letter words either. Fist pumping and being 'down wit da kids' works well for some teachers. For me, I would sound like Julie Andrews if she were from the Midlands, trying to do an impression of Ali Gee. There is never any need to think you need to be 'not you' to be a teacher – or deal with behaviour. As my PGCE tutor, Dr Steve Roberts, taught me: "there are many types of pupils, so we need many types of teachers."

Within my community I have opened this discussion further through the project *Behaviour and YOU!* In which I invite my Inspiring Educators to share experiences of how they feel their identity affects the way they can form positive relationships and support challenging behaviour. My belief is that there is more for us to learn here and we will all benefit from sharing. See Further Reading for how to get involved.

CHECK IN REGULARLY

One of the key aspects to challenging behaviour is that it can be (seemingly) unpredictable. From the outside, behaviour can seem unnecessarily extreme – you take a pupil's phone as per the school rules and they throw a chair at you. Or it may seem to come out of the blue – everyone is working well when suddenly Wayne throws his head down, swears loudly and refuses to engage for the rest of the lesson. The key here is the "seems".

Behaviour is communication, it is never arbitrary.

Do not be mistaken however, this does *not* mean that pupils will always know why they are acting like they are when you ask them; we can't expect this, we don't always know ourselves. Ever found yourself snapping or unfairly judging others? It's not until you catch yourself doing it that you realise that you forgot to eat breakfast.

So if us, as the adults, can't fully understand or predict challenging behaviour, and neither can the pupils, what do we do?

Check in regularly; below is the why, read on for the how.

Regularly over a term, a week, a day, a lesson – depending on your role within school – checking in overtly has a few advantages:

- It forces the pupil (and maybe yourself) to regularly have an opportunity to be honest with themselves. Evaluate actions, events and moods. From this place of knowledge, you can both take account of this information when moving forwards with the learning, knowing whether a transitionary activity is needed or they're ready to learn – saving time in the long run.
- It gives the pupils a structured place they know they will be heard; importantly, without your judgement. We mustn't judge or discourage a child from *feeling* angry, that is a vital human experience. Acting on it and carrying out destructive or harmful action is a separate issue. *Listen* to the feelings and emotions under the actions – without judgement – and you have the key to where your

learning can go that lesson, perhaps alongside consequences that need to be actioned.

- It role models positive communication, which can prevent many a drama. If you know a pupil is upset already, it may not be the time to discuss their latest bad test result with them – what would that gain? We are not here to break children or crush them when they're down. How would that help their engagement in learning or education?

CHECK IN ACTIVITIES AND MODELS

Now the how, on how to fit in check in activities – with very little planning or preparation required:

- During a register, instead of pupils answering "Yes Miss/Mx/Sir" ask them to give one word about their mood. In two minutes, you can gauge a class of 35 – gold dust if you were wondering whether to get the paints out that lesson or not.
- During a test or mock exam provide whiteboards or recycled paper. At the beginning, a point in the middle and at the end of the test, ask pupils to write down one word that describes how they're feeling about the test. I have captured these over several mocks over Year 10 and Year 11 exams, and then before the 'real thing' reflected on the pupils' journey with them, helping them realise how, even though they feel nervous, they are much more equipped and ready than they were three, six, months ago. Studies have proved that the more self-confident we feel before an exam, the more likely we are to do well (Frances-White, 2018).
- For particularly volatile or vulnerable pupils, check in with a consistent key worker at the top ends of each day. This should not be the child's teacher, but someone separate from the formal learning. This member of staff can relay messages or cause for concern to other members of staff, as well as passing on information from home.
- Half termly check ins. In the Finnish model, schools must have a Curator (often translated as counsellor, but not necessarily in the therapeutic sense) for every 500 pupils – by law (as well as a Psychotherapist, School Social Worker and School Nurse – see Further Reading). They meet *every* pupil individually at the start of the year, then schedule in approximately termly/six monthly sessions. The focus is on how learning and school are going, and aspirations for the future and career; the pupil can request an additional session at any time.

It is easy to see: if we get the chance to air worries and challenges, we are *preventing* challenging behaviour. Whether it's later that lesson or in the school journey as a whole.

FOLLOW THEIR LEAD

As mentioned, pupils with challenging behaviour may not present as if they want to get to know you initially – and for some, for a very long time. For the adult trying to make a connection this can quickly become frustrating and dispiriting. If you are not careful, you may find yourself expressing this frustration as you feel the sense of rejection yourself. A regular practice of self-reflection (as discussed in Chapter 1) becomes vital here. Your own sense of rejection is an area for you to explore. Putting this onto the pupil, whether consciously or not, will only further increase their resistance towards you – and may result in you resorting to heavy handed punishment to 'get back' at the pupil for the negativity they are provoking within you. If this is the case, it is important to talk to trusted colleagues or call out for support.

Whilst there are some pupils who are likely to never welcome you with open arms, over time you can do small things to help them gain the trust they need. If it is safe for you both, allow the pupils to have that sense of control as you build a working relationship together, for example giving them choices over their learning – "we've got timestables to do and spellings, which would you like to do this lesson?" – it is a simple choice with few consequences, but the action of giving them agency over their own learning shows that *you* trust them, which sends the signal that you view them as a trustworthy person.

For a child who is used to always being told what to do, or more likely what *not* to do, this trust and respect may feel alien. Some may not know what to do with this trust and grunt at you with 'I dunno' or the like. It's a rinse and repeat exercise – it once took me a full academic year for a pupil to set foot in the library I had set up at his school. Every time I saw him walk past, I would invite him in, usually to the response of "F*** off Miss". Then one day I needed some shelves moving. I asked him for help – showing that *despite* his usual hostile response to me, that I trusted him, I thought he was capable. He came and helped me, during that I introduced some very casual conversations about the books themselves and reading. A few weeks later he wandered into the library himself, "OK Miss, what's it all about in here then?"

Another way to follow their lead is to observe them with other members of staff that they already have a solid relationship with. Speak to that member of staff – sometimes, if you are introduced via someone they already trust a special osmosis of "fine, I'll give them a go" happens. This works particularly well if the pupil has a key worker within the school.

Observing pupils in different settings can also be revealing. If appropriate, join in too – if it's not your subject then *they* have the upper hand. I was taught how to change a drill bit by a pupil – a pupil who had been excluded from three mainstream schools due to behaviour. They loved having the responsibility of teaching me, because *they* were appropriately in control of the situation. Back in your own classroom it gives you something to refer to – "Thanks Jo for teaching me that the other day" – enabling you to recall positive experiences and show them that they have had a lasting positive effect on you. Then, if you are asking them to do something they find hard, you can refer to them helping you as a model of learning: "Jo, when you helped me with that drill bit, did I get it right straight away? And what would have happened if I had just thrown the drill on the floor?"

DON'T TAKE IT FOR GRANTED

Once you have established a positive relationship with a pupil, don't take it for granted that it will always be there. A lot of things can happen in a child's life that can seem huge; and whilst some may act like adults they are still learning. Adult-style sarcasm can be a tricky point. I have observed colleagues learn this the hard way, when they have used sarcasm with a child they thought ready to handle it, who instead took comments personally, breaking the trust cycle of the relationship which meant having to start from scratch to re-build.

USE LEARNING AS COMMON GROUND

Sometimes I hear teachers say that the 'relationship bits' would be nice *if I had time*, which re-enforces the myth that this is an either/or situation and that relationship building is entirely in contrast to formal learning.

MYTH BUSTER: The two are intertwined, just ask supply teachers. Engaging a class *with* formal learning without a former relationship can be hard work (see Further Reading). You might get away with it for a while with classes who have few behaviour needs, but it is not my general experience of teaching in large comprehensive schools and it's obvious why. That manager who repeatedly calls you 'Sady' when you've told them repeatedly it's Sadia? Harder to get motivated to work for them, isn't it? There's a question of respect, and more basically – humanity.

I had a very shy girl in one Year 8 class, Elsie. Whilst she would never be classed as having specific behaviour needs, her timidity and general lack of confidence meant she often didn't participate in learning – she refused to join in with class discussions, group work, unless she was partnered with a friend, and if I forgot to check in with her near the start of the lessons, I would often find she had made little progress as she'd misunderstood a key concept and been too scared to ask for help.

Despite her behaviour not being 'problematic' for me or others socially, the effect was the same – little learning took place.

I needed to build a positive relationship with her, make her feel safe and included before she would feel comfortable enough to ask for help or work with others. The key this time was free writing.

FREE WRITING

Free writing is stream of consciousness, journal writing, gibberish. I have written and vlogged a lot about the ways to approach it, how to do it, differentiate it and use it successfully in the classroom for building relationships, wellbeing *and* academic progress (see Further Reading).

One week, I learnt through Elsie's free writing that she had a hockey tournament that weekend; I made a point of remembering that. The following Monday as I stood at the threshold doing my #ShakeyHandGang I asked her how the tournament went. She was thrilled and flabbergasted. She'd forgotten she'd written about it and knew for certain she hadn't told me. It was the signal she'd needed to know that I saw her and that I cared. After that, she increasingly engaged in my lessons, asked for support when needed and by the end of the year I was happy to do a positive phone call home celebrating with her parents that she now joined in group discussions.

Building positive relationships is essential to academic progress.

PACE

In the UK special schools and PRUs often work separately from mainstreams within the same Local Authority. I find this a great shame, as there is so much good practice in each that, if shared, would help pupils navigate from one to another, and for some perhaps prevent exclusions. One of these practices is PACE, an approach coined by Clinical Psychologist Dan Hughes (Moore, 2020a):

Playfulness

Acceptance

Curiosity

Empathy

Based on Hughes' studies into Attachment Theory (more on this in Chapter 4) and his extensive work with children, parents and carers, PACE gives adults a framework with which to engage with young people and establish reciprocal relationships, particularly with those who have experienced trauma.

Educational Psychologist Dr Chris Moore shares a series of four detailed blogposts on how this formula can be used in the classroom. I will highlight here the key points. PACE is something I return to regularly in my own practice, always with surprisingly successful results.

PLAYFULNESS

Playfulness is all about the positive spectrum of emotions. It is used to elicit moments of shared joy and delight. It can be easy to forget playfulness when we are helping children to tolerate and regulate more difficult emotions, such as anger, terror and envy. (Moore, 2020a)

Moore explains that playfulness is not usually the first approach we use with a child who has difficulty building relationships – before they know you as an adult, they are unlikely to trust any forms of play. Most of us have experienced this at some point – the attempted banter on first meeting with a class? Not always the best introduction; however, used later the shared sense of play and gaming can be greatly beneficial.

In the second week of working in an SEMH school that was in Requires Improvement Ofsted rating at the time, I witnessed an exemplary practice of this by a colleague. I had been working with a pupil who had begun to get very frustrated. We were coming up to half term, and I knew their homelife was not a positive one; anxiety was high. Not knowing the pupil well, I was unable to help them to calm down, I did not understand what had triggered them in the first place, and the situation escalated – the pupil began to rip apart the chair they were sitting on. Feeling trapped, alone and intimidated in my small space, I had to call in for support.

Robert Archard, the Assistant Head and Behaviour Lead, came to help. Having a longstanding relationship with the pupil he was able to use play immediately. This was a refreshing and surprising turn from the atmosphere that the pupil and I had got ourselves into; which was partly why it worked. Robert approached the pupil jovially with a light tone and suggested that a timer was put on to see who could pick up the most bits of sponge from the chair the quickest. I stood, completely bamboozled, as I watched what had been an extremely aggressive pupil suddenly melt, laugh... and tidy up?

After witnessing this mini-behaviour-miracle, I experienced a sense of failure on my part. Why hadn't I thought of this? Why had I not been able to divert the situation in such a successful way? I spoke with Robert afterwards, who explained that he knew the young person well, he could only take that 'risk' of bringing in play into a tense situation due to their established relationship. It was not personal against me, a lesson we forget and return to often as teachers (more on this in Chapter 6).

ACCEPTANCE

Moore describes acceptance as being the most important factor of PACE. "Acceptance is about understanding that the thoughts and feelings underneath the behaviour are not right or wrong" (Moore, 2020b). Whilst this can be extremely challenging for an adult – the child has just set light to their work, they have just spat at you, or hurt another pupil – it doesn't make it any less true: behaviour is communication of thoughts and feelings – those in themselves need acceptance if the child is able to move past their actions. "Acceptance is fundamentally about telling the child, verbally and non-verbally, 'I get it. This is a big deal for you'" (Moore, 2020b). This does not mean that we become lenient about negative actions – consequences, setting limits and discipline are vital, but "Acceptance is about being mindful of the child's past and how that resulted in the behaviour we see today" (Moore, 2020b).

A poignant example: a child is a refugee who has recently escaped a war zone – fighting, stealing and aggression may have been the behaviours they *needed* to adopt in order to eat, in order to survive. The transition from that primal instinct into a peaceful society where the necessities of life are readily available will not be instant. They will need to un-learn behaviours that formerly were not just acceptable but necessary. If we are not careful, our unconscious bias (both as individuals and systemically) may result in overly strict punishments towards young people who have learnt what culture and society is and behavioural expectations in a war zone. It is the child who is then punished, and will take that personally, for something that they had no control over (more on this in Chapter 7).

Acceptance is not easy or instant. You may experience several layers and weeks of rejection, hence why self-care is so important (see Chapter 1).

Acceptance is also hard because we are keen to change behaviour, either to suit our own purposes or to discourage the child from inappropriate or unsafe behaviour. However, when a child has lacked the experience of a caregiving adult accepting and co-regulating their thoughts and feelings, the immediate attempt to change what they are doing can breed further mistrust [...]

Acceptance activates the social engagement system of the brain and decreases defensiveness. (Moore, 2020b)

In practice, acceptance can look like acknowledging the feelings before the action when addressing inappropriate behaviour: "I can see that you are upset that Ms Petrov is not in today, we need to pick up your pens from the floor though now."

CURIOSITY

Curiosity is non-judgemental – it's about exploring and understanding, as opposed to trying to change or correct the other's person experience of a situation. Fundamentally, it enables us to gain new perspectives on the reasons behind a person's words and actions. (Moore, 2020c)

When we notice a pupil's negative behaviour, it is tempting and often instinctive to try to fix it, to put it right. The approach of curiosity invites us to find out *why* the behaviour may have occurred in the first place – what is the pupil feeling? What have they experienced? What do they understand about a particular situation? Once we understand a root cause we are more likely to be able to make appropriate responses, differentiate and prevent negative actions in the future.

Moore explains that, for a child who has not had the chance to explore safely or been encouraged to be curious at an early age, a common response is avoidance; it is safer to avoid than try something new (Moore, 2020c). You will see the effects of this regularly in your classroom – pupils who disrupt or become over anxious rather than try something that they might fail at. As teaching staff, it is important to understand *why* they might be experiencing this; sweeping positive statements "come on, it will be fine" are unlikely to be helpful. Be curious – what is the block for the child? To them it will be very real. If we attempt to change them as a first point of call, it reinforces the message that they are not good enough without the changes made by you, further weakening their self-image.

EMPATHY

Empathy is about 'feeling with', while sympathy is about 'feeling for' [...] It's an active and genuine desire to understand the emotion and validate the emotion without judgement. [...] Empathy enables us to relate better to others. (Moore, 2020d)

Empathy is key to building relationships with pupils who may find this challenging, and if the child has not had many positive opportunities to build positive relationships in their life so far, it will be the adult's role to model this. When a young person does not experience the reconciliation needed to feel accepted once again, they go into a feeling of shame and toxic stress. The focus is inward, on survival, there is little room for considering others in this moment – they have not been considered themselves when distraught, and so this is not a behaviour they are able to learn from others. In the classroom this reveals itself as mistrust and lack of understanding of others. A pupil may be violent towards another and struggle to understand what the other pupil might feel about that.

Moore (2020d) gives examples of how you can show empathy and role model it in the classroom: through your eyes, facial expression and tone of voice – whilst narrating some of the feelings you think they are experiencing. You can then continue to mix this with curiosity and try to get more specific about the situation. You can also show empathy when they are struggling to work things out or take on information about the consequences of their behaviour. Judge a situation appropriately and respond with sincerity.

Again, Moore re-iterates the importance of seeking empathy ourselves as educators who work with vulnerable pupils. We will often take on their negative emotions; they may trigger insecurities or memories of our own that we must be supported with. At these points it is essential that you seek support and continually maintain and refresh your own self-care, as discussed in Chapter 1.

Interview

> Knowing is not the same as being. We can 'know' that building relationships is what gets you the best impact in education, but that's not the same as having a way of being that means I understand that when I smile at you and I look at you, I'm offering us an opportunity.

Lisa Cherry, an author, trainer and speaker on trauma, recovery and resilience, brings thirty years of experience working in education, social care settings, criminal justice and health. Lisa's research in her Master's in Education looked at the intersection of school exclusion and being in care, and the impact upon education and employment across the life course. This research is being continued as a Doctorate at Oxford University. I have attended several of Lisa's trainings and have been deeply moved by the way she intertwines her thorough research with such heartfelt personal experiences.

> The way we think about relationships needs a little unpicking and often that can be because people don't necessarily understand the complexity of how to make relationships because maybe, they've had straightforward relationships. The very notion that somebody might not have those strong relationships is really difficult for people to consider.

She goes on to emphasise that we all arrive in the classroom with our own perspectives and understanding of the world – which affects how we view relationships.

(Continued)

We might say that building relationships is about having a connection between you and me that enables me to feel safe enough to release oxytocin, to feel warmth and connection so that I can hear what you're saying. Or we might say that building relationships is about me feeling safe enough with you; we're talking about emotional safety – I feel like you're not going to harm me, humiliate me, shame me, punish me or do stuff to me. We might have to do that dance a few times of whether it's safe enough, by me just testing you out a bit to see if that's going to work. Then if I feel safe enough, my system is calm enough for me to be able to hear what you're actually saying to me.

For teachers who are less experienced, she gave a great tip of practicing these skills, even online, with trusted colleagues to feel these things that we might not necessarily have personal experience of. For example, shouting vs. bringing the volume down; experiencing what that feels like, noticing what happens in the body: what's that tightening in my chest? Why do I feel like I want to get away?

Moving onto the foundations of relationship building:

There are fundamental things that support relationship building early on: curiosity, being respectful, having boundaries, having consistency. If you say you're going to show up, show up; if you say you're going to do something, do it.

One of the most important things about building relationships is the repair element. When we have those times where we get it wrong, where that boundary gets blurred, the key then is what do we do with that? How do we repair that situation? How do we say sorry? Are we any good at saying sorry? That's a really easy way of taking responsibility and showing enough vulnerability for relationship building in a professional capacity; enough vulnerability for a connection – that's the amber-nectar.

Learning takes place within the relationship.

I asked Lisa how she would respond to the often-heard rhetoric that we don't have time to build relationships within our schools, or that that is a 'softer' approach to teaching. Lisa answered by demonstrating a thought piece she uses in her training:

Think about the teacher that you remember, what is it that you remember about that teacher and what is it that you remember feeling around that teacher? It's most likely that what you will remember is that you loved that subject because of that teacher, or you remember feeling that you were really good at what you were doing because of how that person made you feel. This can sometimes be enough to help people realise that it is those relationships that actually give us the best learning opportunities.

One of the most distressing divisions that we have seen in this conversation is that somehow being relational is not about boundaries and consistency.

> The children and young people who benefit the most from relational approaches need boundaries and consistency if the school is the safe space, if the teacher is the safe relationship.

> This isn't boundaryless, this is actual responsibility for your practice, it's consciousness, it's awareness and it's actual responsibility for your boundaries.

In Lisa's own educational journey, she was excluded from two secondary schools and was in care herself – which is relevant, as children in care are more likely to be excluded. I asked her what qualities the teachers had who she remembers helping her: "the people I remember the most vividly were the teachers who sort of had some kind of emotional connection with me." In secondary schools, despite being an A grade student, Lisa started to have problems in school.

> The challenge is, when you are in care, you are probably moving around a lot and you're also dealing with fractured relationships, at the same time as having very little ability to actually articulate what's actually going on for you. I also had lots of difficulties, as lots of children do who are experiencing or have experienced trauma, lots of difficulties with relationships and friendships. That's really difficult because it's friendships that make the difference, and yet it's connecting and having friendships that's the hardest thing for children who are struggling, because you have to be vulnerable.

This honest sharing affirms to us that the pupils who we may have the most difficulty forming a positive relationship with are the ones who are in need of it the most – they are not experiencing these connections elsewhere. Forming positive connections needs to be taught, practiced and role modelled explicitly within our schools.

Lisa left school with no O levels; despite this, she went on to get a degree, Masters and now a Doctorate. Which leads us onto Lisa's final reflection on the focus on relationships within education:

> When we don't support people to have their basic qualifications and their basic learning, it has a huge impact on self-esteem and confidence; you can't access anything else without it. We have a balance in how we build those relationships whilst at the same time building that educational resilience that creates a difference across the life course for that person.

> All that I'm talking about today is embedded in rich research. There is no research to show that it will really benefit a child to be locked in a room on their own. There is no research that will show you that if I can't self-regulate and you punish me for not being able to self-regulate that I'm going to learn how to self-regulate. There is no research on that.

> Source: Interview with author, 2020

Action Box

Next lesson

Include a check in activity at the start of the lesson. What do you learn from it? How can it improve your differentiation for your pupil or class that lesson?

Next week

Continue with your check in activity, tweak if necessary, from what you learnt last week. How are the pupils reacting now? How does the repetition affect their attitude towards it? What differences are you noticing in their responses and how does that play out during the lesson and their progress with the work?

Long term

Choose one or maximum two pupils whose behaviour you find challenging.

Over a period of 4–6 weeks apply the PACE approach.

Keep a record of your reflections or better still share with a colleague – or even share over on Twitter using the hashtag #EduTwitter and tag me in, @adelebatesZ. Actually do this (go and get that journal now, I'll wait for you), you never remember as much as you think you will. You could focus on a different aspect of PACE each week – re-reading the notes on each part as a reminder at the start of the week (starting with Acceptance first is advisable).

What do you learn about the pupil? What do you learn about their behaviour? What are they trying to communicate with it? What do you learn about your teaching approach? What do they teach you? How can you adapt your learning to better accommodate their needs? What successes can you celebrate with them?

What has any of this got to do with behaviour?

Building positive relationships is essential to long term behaviour management and learning engagement – especially for those who have not had such relationships outside of school. To successfully build relationships with pupils, we need to be consistent and kind over a sustained period of time.

Further reading

The Still Face Experiment – Dr Edward Tronick

In this short article by Mary Gregory (2020) there is a three-minute video demonstrating Dr Tronick's experiment – how a primary carer's reactions can influence the emotional development of a baby. https://psychhelp.com.au/what-does-the-still-face-experiment-teach-us-about-connection/ (accessed March 26, 2021).

Kith: The Riddle of the Childscape – Jay Griffiths (2014)

Whilst travelling the world for her other book *Wild*, Griffiths became interested in the different environments children grow up in in different cultures. With stark contrasts to other countries, it show how the Western way is not the only way and puts into serious question whether we have got it right for nurturing our next generation.

Connection before Correction – Kim S. Golding CBE

Based on a presentation for the Childhood Trauma Conference, this paper examines the complex behaviour that children can display when they have experienced traumatic homelives and demonstrates the effects it can have on their development. www.researchgate.net/publication/276500716_Connection_Before_Correction_Supporting_Parents_to_Meet_the_Challenges_of_Parenting_Children_who_have_been_Traumatised_within_their_Early_Parenting_Environments (accessed March 26, 2021).

Establishing relationships quickly with pupils you don't usually work with – Adele Bates

https://adelebateseducation.co.uk/establishing-relationships-quickly-with-pupils-you-dont-usually-teach/ (accessed March 26, 2021).

A free, easy tool to support wellbeing AND academic progress – Adele Bates

https://adelebateseducation.co.uk/a-free-easy-tool-to-support-wellbeing-and-academic-progress/ (accessed March 26, 2021).

Free writing for all – Adele Bates

https://adelebateseducation.co.uk/free-writing-for-all/ (accessed March 26, 2021).

All of these blog posts go into further detail for topics touched upon in this chapter. You can find further articles on my website: adelebateseducation.co.uk/blog

To find out more about the *Behaviour and YOU!* Project and to get involved, check out https://adelebateseducation.co.uk/introducing-behaviour-and-you/ (accessed March 26, 2021).

4

"MISS, YOU DON'T EVEN KNOW ME": SEE THE CHILD, NOT THE BEHAVIOUR

#INSULTOFTHEWEEK

Pupil: "What does catastrophe mean?"

Me: "It's similar to a disaster."

Pupil: "Oh, like this lesson then."

(He went on to do the most work he's done for me – ever.)

IN THIS CHAPTER YOU WILL

- Understand that negative behaviour is communication of an unmet need.
- Get an introduction to attachment awareness and how that can help improve behaviour in your classroom.

INTRODUCTION

It is hard to always see the 'child', especially when that child is a foot taller than you and, in that beautifully ugly-duckling-adolescent style, doesn't always know how to keep control of their upper limbs – or bowels. It is also hard when they're swearing at you, destroying things, harming themselves, others, or you and intentionally picking at the scab of your own weak spot – your newly sprouting grey hairs, for example.

It is hard in these circumstances, and hence why 'See the child, *not* the behaviour' becomes such an important mantra.

In order to keep this open approach in mind – even in heightened, challenging situations – we can be curious about what is behind the behaviour, what the behaviour is trying to communicate and what might be causing it.

BEHAVIOUR AS COMMUNICATION

In her book, *Inside I'm Hurting*, Bombèr (2007) repeatedly advocates that behaviour is communication; we know that ourselves – you may have a partner, family member, housemate (or maybe it's you) who gets grumpy before they eat.

The behaviour = I'm angry, leave me alone

In contrast, the message = feed me

Even as grown adults we are often unable to articulate exactly what we wish to communicate in the moment. For teenagers, whose brains are experiencing a unique elasticity, it's a bigger challenge. If, in addition, the young person has SEMH, SEND or other communication issues, the challenge is heightened. In my experience, adults understand this conundrum in toddlers a lot more easily. When a toddler is teething, you tend to know about it (as do the neighbours), and whilst it is frustrating, it is understood:

The behaviour = screaming, hitting etc.

The message = I'm in pain, I don't understand it, make it stop

So often with our vulnerable teenagers the same pattern is at play, and yet we treat it differently. It is our job as educators to remember this. Of course, expectations of teenagers in comparison to toddlers will be different, this is not an excuse to let pupils get away with 'bad behaviour'. However, understanding a similar communication breakdown is at play will help us in the long term with our relationship and ultimately our ability to help these pupils learn.

Why does the communication breakdown occur in the first place? Why are *some* pupils able to articulate this clearly?

ATTACHMENT AWARENESS

The main theory, initially investigated by Bowlby in the 1960s, suggests that the relationship a child has with their primary caregiver during the first three years of their life can create patterns that re-occur in adolescence and adulthood. If those relationships do not foster a positive bond or attachment, then there can be negative consequences in the child's future behaviour – which will often stand in the way of their education.

For pupils who have experienced severe trauma, abuse or neglect – or even been a very young carer for ill parents or carers – there has sometimes not been the opportunity to form these secure attachments, and thus they are communicated later on as behaviour needs.

WHAT DOES IT LOOK LIKE IN SCHOOL?

There are three main areas of attachment disorders as outlined by Bombèr. Some of the possible signs are listed below:

AVOIDANT ATTACHMENT

- outwardly the child is eager to please
- internally they may be feeling anxiety
- value achievements and accomplishments more than intimate relationships
- can be socially uncomfortable
- control things when they can to feel safer
- pain can be internalised as sickness
- aggression can build up
- seeks to meet their own needs
- often related to a depressed or abusive caregiver (Bombèr, 2007)

What it looks like in the classroom:

Ivan, 12 years old, gets very excited when he receives a reward – yet when teachers try to praise him, he struggles to accept it. He doesn't have many friends; dinner supervisors have said they have seen him trying to talk or play with others, but he doesn't fully understand the social cues that the others give him; he often mentions having a pain in his stomach but seems content to deal with it on his own; he seems confused when staff try to give him sympathy. He can become easily distracted from his work, and yet he is capable which is frustrating for his teachers.

AMBIVALENT ATTACHMENT

- clings to a specific adult to attempt to get their needs met
- can become addicted to getting attention from caregiver in order to survive
- often related to an inconsistent caregiver
- interrupts and talks a lot – can be tiring to work with (Bombèr, 2007)

What it looks like in the classroom:

Fran, 15 years old, has recently become very clingy. She waits at her teacher's classroom door at the start of every break, and sometimes after school. She comes to sit right next to the teacher and often sings silly songs on repeat, mainly when she is asked a question that she wants to ignore. She is constantly fiddling with something and recently broke a school stapler. Her teacher is finding her quite annoying.

DISORGANISED ATTACHMENT

* volatile, unpredictable behaviours
* unsafe behaviour
* result of chaotic, neglect, terrifying and/or abusive environment
* they expect the worse
* try to stay in control
* low self-awareness (Bombèr, 2007)

What it looks like in the classroom:

Adiliah, 8 years old, has been isolating herself in the classroom for the last couple of weeks. She is picking fights with other pupils regularly without apparent reason. She will settle to do some work, but only if she's sat on her own. The Teaching Assistant working with her says that he never knows what's going to happen, her language can also be aggressive quite suddenly – he feels he always needs to be on alert with her.

Any form of attachment disorder will affect communication – the challenging behaviour is more likely to come first, as that is the only way the pupil has learnt to communicate. Some of those seemingly negative communications may have actually been successful in the past from the child's perspective – a child whose early years were spent with an ill parent may have learnt that they had to be 'bad' before they were given any attention. From the parent's point of view, if the child seemed to be getting on OK, there were more pressing health issues to deal with – only when the child did something negative, did they realise the child needed attention. The child has therefore learnt that to get attention from an adult, the most successful strategy is to do something negative or become a challenge to the adult.

SHAME AND EMPATHY

A child with attachment disorders often has issues dealing with extreme experiences of shame. Even in positively attached relationships shame is part of the learning process about behaviour. As Golding (2015) explains, children develop feelings of shame when parents begin to put boundaries in place. If a child were to jump into the road, the parent might sternly pull them back and tell them not to do it again. At that moment the relationship has become disconnected and the child feels shame. In a securely attached relationship the parent then repairs the relationship by either showing or telling the child that everything is OK. In insecure attachments this reparation section is missing, the child sits in the shame, feels the loss of the relationship and is unable to regulate their emotion.

The experience of shame builds up into toxic unregulated shame which influences the children's developing sense of identity; the children develop a sense of being bad. The children have to develop a shield to defend against how bad this feels. This shield against shame is demonstrated through a range of behaviours including lying, blaming others, minimizing and raging. (Golding, 2015: 4–5)

It is at these moments – during the lying, blame, withdrawing and rage – that we experience challenging behaviour.

SHAME IN SCHOOLS

I was on a short school trip to a nearby park with a group of KS3 boys from an Alternative Provision. All the students were there for some reason linked to SEMH, nearly all showed evidence of attachment issues. (For tips on running your own school trip with SEMH pupils, see Further Reading.)

It can be a nerve-racking expedition stepping into a public space with young people who have the potential at any time to call out "Go lick your dead Gran". In this instance the park was huge, and luckily it was a quiet, hot day. The pupils could let off steam – and we didn't have to endure judgemental looks, eye rolls and tusks from passing dog walkers.

On the return to the coach a few pupils decided to climb over an iron fence. The final one couldn't quite manage it. I had worked with this pupil for a while, I knew that he had a challenging home life and went to regular respite foster care. In the past few weeks, he had rapidly grown to now tower over me, he was also quickly learning how to be 'well-hard'. The little boy – with the reading age of an 8-year-old, who I often had the honour of meeting in our one-to-one sessions, was being given increasingly less air time, and yet the struggle between these two characters was notable – as they both lived in this one, gangly awkward teenage body.

He asked me to give him a leg up. There was no real danger in this, it was a sense of adventure hung over from the previous park activities. We'd had a great time – discovering an abandoned 'haunted' house, and the pupils (all of whom were at least 13 years old) genuinely believed that we were the first ones to encounter it.

I was keen to continue the spirit of the day – offsite trips can be fun for the grown-ups too. Unfortunately though this particular task was a step too far for me: 'legs up' and climbing in general is not my field of expertise; I am pretty useless at it, but I could see how much this boy wanted to go the same way as his mates. I tried to help him – clasping my, what now appeared to be tiny delicate hands, as a platform for his huge muddy boy-man foot. I failed abysmally. The first boys had since run to the coach, leaving this pupil to have to walk around the fence – with me.

He was angry.

He was angry that he had failed.

He was angry that he had lost face in front of his mates.

He was angry that he'd had to ask for help in the first place and he was angry that the only person who could have helped him was useless at this task.

He felt ashamed.

He expressed this anger initially by throwing his water over me. As it was a boiling hot day and we had had a water fight previously, I felt it best to laugh that off, keep my distance from him for a bit and enjoy the cool down.

The next day however, things turned. I called the pupil in for his session with me. It was clear that he was still angry.

> The behaviour = swearing at me, threatening me, hitting me with his skateboard

> The message = I am ashamed you saw me fail, you saw my weakness and I don't know how to deal with that. You made me feel small, so I will try to make you feel small – I don't know how else to handle this emotion

As the pupil was 'in red' at this stage, it was best to take myself away from the situation and pass on to another member of staff. That sentence sounds very clean – sometimes it can be, but it can also be scary. Aggression and violence are threatening by nature – and frustratingly for me in this moment, the other staff member was a despondent Teaching Assistant who – *during* the altercation – began to recite the ills of the school: "you shouldn't have been left alone with him without a radio, the consequences aren't strong enough in this school." He wasn't actually interacting with the pupil but droning directly at me. It was a tough call; would he be able to handle the pupil any better? Unlikely, but in this heightened moment *I* was his target, I was being hurt physically – the boy hadn't even noticed the running commentary of the failure of the education system. So I left, and sent help in as fast as I could.

Despite being a target, the behaviour was not personal (more on this in Chapter 6). My very face had reminded the pupil of the previous day's events. It most likely triggered all the other times in his life where he had felt embarrassed, ashamed or like a failure – of which I happened to know unfortunately there had been many.

Later, in his session with the on-site therapist, my suspicions were confirmed. He had, in that safe, explorative environment, been able to identify how he had been feeling, and then express his guilt towards his aggression towards me. Even more impressively, he was able to realise that apologising to me was the proper thing to do.

Seeing the child and not the behaviour was vital to me being able to re-build our relationship. If I had taken his aggressive behaviour as the message out of context it would have been:

> The behaviour = swearing at me, threatening me, hitting me with his skateboard

> The message = I hate you, I want to hurt you

> My sensible human response = get away from this threat, fight back and/or punish

To merely punish this behaviour without seeing the child and their situation underneath would have caused the rift between us to widen as, on top of the already quickly building negativity, he would have reason to hold a grudge towards me for the punishment.

Instead, I separated the two things.

I was shaken by a hooded youth hitting me with a skateboard – so once I left him, I immediately informed colleagues (more on this in Chapter 8) and allowed myself some calming down time. I was not seriously hurt, so was able to look at what this child may have been trying to communicate with me; why he might not have been able to regulate his emotions and the confusion, embarrassment and shame that he was experiencing; at the same time knowing that there would need to be a consequence for hitting a member of staff.

By the time he came to apologise to me, he was out of the red (this is essential) and calm enough for me to be able to speak with him and begin repairing the relationship. I thanked him for the apology – I'm always impressed when a pupil (or member of staff) can do this. It is a powerful gesture. I then explained to him that he would still need the consequence for hitting a member of staff. I asked him why he had got so angry and was there anything I had done to upset him. He was slow in expressing to me, so I prompted him by offering the idea that he was still frustrated by the previous day. It was enough for him to put the two together; and I was able to explain to him that being frustrated with my lack of climbing skills was perfectly understandable, but the way he had expressed it was not. I was able to reassure him, that whilst he might feel shame for the violence, that everything was OK. I would still be there for him – I did this by then focusing on the work. The incident was over, I would not mention it again – unless he did, and we could continue to build on our relationship and his learning.

So how do you hold on to this mantra in practice?

It's an ongoing exploration, and we don't always get it right. Much like any relationship, it must be continually nurtured. Listening, learning and exploring are all key.

IN THE CLASSROOM

REMEMBER THE CHILD IS A CHILD

Take some time, when away from the child or class, to imagine the child for who they are: a child. A child who is still learning about the world; a child who may have had adverse or traumatic experiences; a child who is learning how to express themselves and all their complex emotions successfully; a child who needs strong, positive adult role models to help them learn how to do this.

GET TO KNOW YOUR PUPILS

Much like the teething toddler – a passer-by may look over in horror and wonder what has possessed the child. The toddler's parent or carer, however, will hopefully know the patterns and signs, understand what has gone on before with the child, and if they are not able to offer a soothing solution, at least be able to distance themselves from the behaviour, knowing that it will pass – and it is a part of a child's development.

In the same way, the more we know our pupils the more we can do this. The way we know a teenage pupil and the way a person might know their own toddler are different, but the process is the same.

SEE BEHAVIOUR AS COMMUNICATION AND NEGOTIATE

The behaviour could be a thrown bag and a curse word in your direction. What Jemma is communicating is that she wants to sit with Sandhya – it's this part we can negotiate on. Similar to the negotiating we did in Chapter 1 with colleagues, the same framework can be helpful. Understanding the child's needs does not mean doing everything the pupil desires. Sometimes you will both have to make compromises, as in any healthy relationship:

1. Understand: "I know you want to sit with Sandhya, she's a really good friend of yours."
2. Set your boundary: no need to justify yourself, but remember they may genuinely need the reminder: "That won't be possible today, as I mentioned last week, because we're working on something else today."
3. Offer an alternative: "However, next lesson it's group work again and I could take this as a request that you two would like to work together if you like?"
4. Listen: This may be met by protests of unfairness and frustration, repeat the process:

"I know it's frustrating for today (understand), but I know you know this is the seating plan (setting the boundary), we've got our plan for next lesson where you are with Sandhya (offer an alternative), and if today and next lesson go well, I would be happy then to have a conversation with you about a long term solution we're both happy with. Can you work with that?" (Listen).

If at this stage they are unable to engage, then you will need to move to helping them regulate their emotions before continuing. See later in the Chapter 5 for more on this.

In this scenario you may also need to deal with the swearing. I would advise dealing with this, and any consequences, when the pupil is calm, not when you're trying to negotiate a next step.

STEP AWAY WHEN YOU NEED TO

Every so often you will come across that delightful 'one' who just gets under your skin (as I write this I picture the grinning and antagonising face of one of mine). Firstly, that's OK, this is evidence of the fact that you are human – and you are totally forgiven for that. If not a particular pupil, it may be a particular situation, or a particular insult you hear that triggers you on a personal level. In these circumstances, it is best to walk away. You are not the best person to deal with this situation at this time. This doesn't mean that this will always be the case, but if you feel your own anger rise, step away. If the child's behaviour is an attempt to communicate confusion or a lack of something in any way, an angry adult will make the situation worse.

If you are working one-on-one and you are not immediately able to pass on to a colleague, then carve out some space or move both you and the pupil to a public place where you can call to a colleague.

LEARN TO DISTANCE YOURSELF FROM THE BEHAVIOUR

More on this in Chapter 6 – Don't take it personally.

ACCOUNT FOR ADDITIONAL EMOTIONAL STRAIN YOURSELF

If you are the TA or teacher, communicate regularly with colleagues about challenging situations you have been in. If things become overwhelming look for tweaks in a timetable or group that might help. For leaders, consider the additional emotional and mental strain of working with these pupils. Best practice is to have a framework of supervision between staff or counselling available within school, in addition to regular spaces for reflection – for any adult who spends time with these pupils.

GET TRAINED

Being aware of different attachment disorders is a start – it enables us to remember to see the child behind the behaviour and remain curious about the reasons why they may have challenging behaviour for staff. Seek out and provide ongoing training about issues that affect behaviour. Training needs to be ongoing so that staff have space to understand and learn from the daily challenges they face.

Interview

> Be a detective and translator, rather than an enforcer – ask, what is this behaviour telling me?

Frédérique Lambrakis-Haddad has over 25 years of experience working as a Child and Adolescent Therapist with young people in socio-economically deprived and ethnically diverse areas in the UK and the US. She is now a Freelance Consultant at Traumainform.com, supporting organisations and individuals' capacity to address past adverse experiences and to support an environment which helps builds resilience and self-sufficiency.

Frédérique has worked for 15 years as the lead clinician and senior leader in primary and secondary Brighton and Hove schools for students with Social, Emotional and Mental Health challenges.

Frédérique begins by warning us:

> It's easy to get distracted by the behaviour and not look at the child. The key is to look at what is underlying it, the communication. [She explains to us that] behaviour that we are witnessing as maladaptive (stressful, frightening, aggressive, unkind) in our school environments, would have been survivalist behaviour in a maladaptive (difficult) environment. So in fact the child's behaviour is adaptive, they're only maladaptive when you take them to a more healthy environment.

An example of this would be stealing food – in a home where the child was not regularly fed, they have developed stealing behaviour in order to physically survive, which is a suitable behaviour in this environment. When that behaviour comes into school, this survivalist behaviour has not changed, but now it is being labelled as wrong, as the environment is now providing regular food. However, it may take a pupil a long time to trust this new environment. It is important to note too,

> that if a child has what we consider positive behaviours in a maladaptive home, they may not survive; certainly emotionally and possibly physically.

In these situations, Frédérique advises for us to foster a tone of curiosity, rather than consequences, and ask, what is this actually telling me about the young person and their history? We don't need to take it so literally.

> Teachers sometimes think if they're kind, empathic, compassionate that should reach the young person; that can also overwhelm the young person and if they have not been raised in an environment where they can recognise it they're not going to trust it.

I asked Frédérique, given the vast amount of evidence concerning Attachment Theory and trauma informed practice that is now available, how much of that she thought teaching staff on the ground need to know.

> The theory is important, but what is more important is having curiosity, about having boundaries, about not taking insults or behaviours literally but to look at what they're communicating and not to personalise things: have curiosity not judgement. What I think we should all be trained in more is self-awareness. We all come in with our personal baggage, we all get drawn towards certain kids and repelled by other kids. To be curious towards yourself and not judgemental, and then you can actually work on it.

I questioned Frédérique on her view on boundaries:

> Boundaries are a lot more than rules. I think rules take a part of it. Boundaries need to be consistent, as they are containing. So to be a teacher who is predictable and persistent really helps contain. That's why you get some strict teachers who are very successful, because they're containing. If that's not your nature, you might find other ways to contain. Be boringly consistent. Then once you've built the consistency and structure you can be fun within that.

Probing about how strict we should be Frédérique explains:

> I 100% believe that kids pick up on your genuine nature: don't be funny if you're not funny. Sometimes less confident teachers try to replicate what works for someone else; allow your own personality in. A child who has had

(Continued)

a traumatic history, who are the ones likely to be behaving difficultly, will be hypervigilant, and one of the qualities of being hypervigilant is being super attuned to their environment to survive.

The other thing teachers should know about is triggers:

1. They're invisible most of the time – invisible to you. It might be the tick of the clock, it might be where they're sitting, it might be a smell. If they were abused in Halloween time, the smell of wood burning or the sight of a pumpkin might be triggering.
2. They are most likely to be sensory.
3. There are internal *and* external triggers.
4. Most of the time children are not aware of their triggers.
5. A trigger is a threat – the amygdala picks up and goes into danger mode. The pupil is cutting out everything else apart from preservation mode. Most of it is lodged in the body.

Rather than asking a child "what is wrong" you have to get your detective head on. Sit with them *later* and wonder "I've seen you really struggle today, was there something that was going on in the classroom that felt uncomfortable with you? When you started going off did you notice anything happening in your body?" – prompt them to be curious about their bodily state. Then you can put strategies in place to help them regulate – sensory objects can be useful here.

Frédérique finishes by explaining another key concept to help teachers – the Window of Tolerance, which we might read as 'being ready to learn'. The Window of Tolerance has three different strands: the 'window of tolerance' in the middle where you feel comfortable, 'hyperarousal' at the top where you can't calm down and are overreactive, and below the window of tolerance sits 'hypoarousal' where you shut down and are unmotivated. See Further Reading for more information on this.

As teachers we are aiming to get our pupils in the central zone. We all go up and down, when we are triggered, we go into hyperarousal or hypoarousal. If a pupil has been traumatised, their Window of Tolerance is smaller, so they can shift into hyper or hypo arousal more quickly, and they also stay in it longer. That's where the physical, sensory work comes in. That's where the detective comes in again, because different things will work for different people. So having a list of physical grounding techniques can be really helpful.

To end, Frédérique emphasises the importance of preserving ourselves:

I harp on about it a lot: self-awareness and self-care. In my opinion there's loads of domains: physical, emotional, spiritual, relationships and work self-care; these aren't greedy, they'll actually make you a better teacher. You're role modelling to your pupils

Everyone has something positive, they must. So if they're really quite unappealing to you for whatever reasons, then you haven't opened yourself up to seeing that positiveness in them.

Source: Interview with author, 2020

Action Box

Next lesson

Think of an instance where there was some challenging behaviour from a pupil that you felt unable to understand or manage. What was the specific behaviour? What could the message have been, what could they have been trying to communicate?

Talk to a colleague who knows the pupil well – can you find more patterns? Discuss what small support you could try next lesson – a change in seating plan, five minute time out card, positive phone calls home, giving them an outline of the lesson and key words earlier in the day/week.

Try, note what works, try again.

Next week

What do you have built into your teaching practice that allows you to get to know where your pupils are from, from a social, emotional, mental health point of view?

Choose the two to three most challenging pupils you currently work with.

In the next week discover at least two new things about each of them that you didn't know before. This might involve going to see them outside of your class – observe them in a lesson different to yours, particularly in a lesson you know they enjoy or where they have a good relationship with that teacher.

You may have a one-to-one chat with them in another time (form time can be useful) – not about behaviour, but about them – sitting and asking questions can be intense for both parties, and the pupil will be waiting to see what they've 'done wrong'; the chat can be disguised by getting them to do a job for you, something practical so that you don't have to look directly at each other is usually good – make sure they are rewarded for it.

What did you learn? How can this inform your practice?

(Continued)

Long term

This chapter is a short introduction, seek further training around attachment issues, SEMH, trauma informed practice or ACEs (see Chapter 2).

What has any of this got to do with behaviour?

The behaviour is the surface level effect of challenges that obscure a pupil's learning. Making the effort to understand what these challenges might be, remaining open as they may not be what you think they are, and adapting accordingly is differentiation. This is vital if we are to get past a young person's 'bad' behaviour and help them thrive with their education.

Further reading

Worst nightmare? – How to organise a successful school trip (with students who may just possibly swear in public) – Adele Bates
A how to guide to organising school trips for pupils with SEMH and other behavioural needs. Available at: https://adelebateseducation. co.uk/how-to-organise-a-successful-school-trip/

Window of Tolerance
A vlog and blog explanation of the Window of Tolerance and how it can be used in schools. Available at: https://adelebateseducation. co.uk/window-of-tolerance/

CAUTION: Proceed with thought and curiosity – Frédérique Lambrakis-Haddad
A useful blog post for educators delving into trauma informed practice and providing real-life case studies and practical actions for teachers. Available at https://adelebateseducation.co.uk/caution-proceed-with-thought-and-curiosity/

Inside I'm Hurting: Practical Strategies for Supporting Children with Attachment Difficulties in Schools – Louise Michelle Bombèr (2007)

A practical guide that brings Attachment Theory into the classroom. Useful for educators who want to understand more.

Nurturing Children: From Trauma to Growth Using Attachment Theory, Psychoanalysis and Neurobiology – Graham Music (2019)
   Music's book tackles many of the big issues that affect 'troubled' children: trauma, neglect, depression and violence. Through case studies, theory and vast amounts of experience, Music provides approaches to supporting these vulnerable young people.

Escaping Green House – Debra Shaefer
   An essential memoir for any educator to read, Debra's book is due for publication in 2022. I had the honour of reading some early drafts; her intimate sharing will be a game changer in the way we understand our children who have been through trauma:

> I want to tell you the story of my childhood – about a little girl who most probably did not start out as mentally ill but was damaged to the point that she aspired to become a murderer. And I know it might be difficult to read of such things, but my instinct is to be gentle with you, especially when the lesson is difficult. See, I am a teacher, and my life of lies, drugs, incest and insanity might help you understand the lessons I should have learned much sooner than I did.

5

"MISS, BUT I AM BEING QUIET": EXPLICITLY TEACHING BEHAVIOUR AND SELF-REGULATION

#INSULTOFTHEWEEK

Me: "Please put your rubbish in the bag."
Pupil: "You need a much bigger bag."
Me: "Why?"
Pupil: "You won't fit in that one."

IN THIS CHAPTER YOU WILL

- Understand why some pupils need to be taught seemingly obvious things.
- Learn how to teach social behaviours through the ordinary content of subject lessons.

INTRODUCTION

A few years ago, I led some drama lessons in a special SEMH school. The class consisted of around six very high profile pupils who did not get on. Their behavioural needs and negative educational experiences up to this point were such that it was challenging to keep them all in a classroom without bullying and harming one another (and sometimes the staff). They were at the start of secondary school. I introduced activities that would require them to gently work together, with low status risk. Anything physical was a winner: staring competitions (may have gone on for twenty minutes one lesson), pat-your-head-rub-your-tummy, swing-one-arm-back-and-one-arm-forwards. Slowly I brought in increasingly physical activities that involved trusting peers, such as group balances and walking in the style of one another. In between the swearing, frustration and much persuasion from the staff, the pupils experienced some real moments of connection and shared, group focus.

One exercise however, taught me the most: *Are you my friend, are you my enemy?* based on an exercise by Sue Cowley (2001). Put simply, pupils role play scenarios in which they are either friends or enemies. After laying down ground rules (no physical contact, no swearing) I set up some scenes. Acting as enemies was easy, and the non-swearing rule actually proved how wide their vocabulary was. Acting as friends revealed something different however. They couldn't do it. At first I didn't understand what the block was. Naively I thought, how could they *not* know how to make friends? Even when paired with an adult they had a positive relationship with, they couldn't find the words, the body language or the tone of voice. It dawned on me; this was a skill that I needed to explicitly teach, in the same way that I would teach, for example, a poem: model, deconstruct, word level analysis, inference, comparison, questioning and finally re-constructing and own creation. The same process was required here: modelling, deconstructing, explicit teaching of parts, re-construction and own creation. I spent the following weeks dissecting the friend-enemy exercise. I created strips of dialogue; first they had to categorise them into 'friendly' and 'not-friendly' piles. We discussed how they might feel and react to different sentences. They chose three each and attempted to put them back into the friend-enemy scenarios. We explored body language that might match the dialogue. One breakthrough lesson for me, I saw a child using the 'friendly' language whilst shouting at his partner and wondering why it wasn't working. This explained so much. This pupil was often known for shouting, which was linked to many of his behavioural incidents. It was clear through this work that he didn't know *how* to use other strategies of communication to express his unmet needs; it was not through choice that he used this vocal tone, but through *lack* of choice. It was my job to offer and model alternative ways.

> When children don't know how to read, we teach. When they don't know how to write, we teach. When they don't know how to ride a bike, we teach. But when children don't know how to behave, do we teach? Or do we punish? We punish. (Allen, 2016: 9.55)

In mainstream schools in particular, there is an expectation that pupils know how to behave and they choose not to. This is not always the case: "No Sally, you need to *share* the sandpit" – share is an abstract concept. For a child who has not experienced it, it will be impossible to action; the same with such phrases as 'be patient', 'take your turn', 'calm down' and 'behave nicely'.

> What if we taught them how to make friends, how to initiate play, how to take turns and then we gave them many opportunities to practice...and positively reinforced them every time they used those skills. Challenging behaviours would be greatly reduced. (Allen, 2016: 10.20)

HOW DO WE TEACH POSITIVE BEHAVIOUR?

Whenever I get stuck on 'how' to teach these areas I go back to how would I teach a poem (or insert another regular teaching construct in your subject). Model, deconstruct, explicitly teach components, re-construct, opportunities for pupils' own creations. You can apply this to any subject, how *do* you usually teach?

ON POSITIVE BEHAVIOUR: MODEL

Give examples of positive and negative behaviour, comparison can be a useful tool here. These could be videos, role play, scripts. This doesn't have to be an add on, it can be integrated into your subject. PE teachers teach the rules of a game, what a foul looks like etc. In preparation for an exam, we outline the codes of practice, what cheating would look like in this context. In DT or art modelling it may look like a safety lesson with equipment along with consequences of good use and misuse, both in terms of safety, punishments and achievements. You can exemplify past work – when this pupil was able to use the equipment well, they produced this by the end of the term. In history, it may be a lesson on how to debate and discuss, examining the difference between that and an argument. Approach modelling positive behaviour in a similar way – don't assume all your pupils will instinctively know, no matter how old they are.

However, be cautious about instilling norms and value judgements as 'right'. Social and cultural differences will play out here. A more useful discussion is around what's appropriate for different contexts. Bouncing a ball in an exam hall would be (most likely) seen as 'bad behaviour' whereas it is encouraged in basketball. This teaches young people that there are different expectations of behaviour in different places – announcing your engagement to your same-sex partner in one country may lead to celebration, in another country it would lead to death – the behaviour is the same (more on this in Chapter 6).

DECONSTRUCT

As my first example about friendship demonstrated, we can easily assume that pupils know what 'good' looks like. In deconstructing an area, we can learn about the parts of miscomprehension; for example, Sammy may believe that when Isaac lends her a pen that that then means she can use it whenever she wants. Next lesson she takes the pen without asking, and Isaac becomes upset, Sammy has stolen from him.

In an unfortunate situation, Sammy may be triggered at being accused of stealing and react negatively; she pushes Isaac off his chair. You turn around at this point, all you see is Isaac on the floor upset because of Sammy. Deconstructing scenarios with a child with challenging behaviour enables you to understand where the teaching point is – in this instance, to understand what lending means, and then to learn how to express negativity without harming others. In Maths this might look like you giving clearer guidelines on when a calculator can and can't be used, visual reminders may be needed for example – so that if this is ignored, the pupil understands why they might be accused of cheating. In science it could be a discussion or instructions on how to share a Bunsen burner – what does that look like? It was one between four in my secondary school – it was assumed in Year 7 that we knew how to share, and so in my group I never got a go. I wasn't particularly bothered (Physics and Chemistry were my least favourite subjects), instead I would get my lines out that I needed to learn for my next show. I (quite rightly) got told off for doing this, but there was no other investigation into what was happening or why I was doing this. No one asked *why* I was learning my show lines in a science lesson. No one deconstructed what was going on. As a result, I returned to staring out of the window – with no further knowledge or experience of a Bunsen burner (my partner does the camping cooking).

Whilst teaching an SEMH pupil remotely, I noticed, after a couple of sessions, that they were becoming increasingly distracted online. I realised that when this happened, they focused on the bottom right hand side of the screen – they were watching a funny video. I discussed this with the pupil, I highlighted that in this instance (remote learning) that that was not appropriate behaviour and then asked (deconstructed) as to what had made them do this. They had found the work task challenging and needed a break. I then taught them how to deal with and communicate that feeling in a positive way in this remote learning context; telling me and asking for a sensory break. The next lesson they did exactly this. Deconstructing the behaviour in the context provided a solution – the behaviour improved and focus on learning increased.

RECONSTRUCT

In the example above, the reconstruction was teaching the pupil how to communicate appropriately that they needed a break. In the instance with the two children and the pen lending, the reconstruction teaching point would be facilitating discussion around lending and helping Sammy to either come to a new understanding of the social etiquette around lending in this society, or facilitating a conversation with Isaac on what the arrangement should look like moving forwards. For reconstruction it is essential, as the adult, that we let go of what negativity *did* happen and focus on *how could this work more positively next time?* Sometimes we're not ready for that ourselves. If a pupil has hit or upset us emotionally there is a forgiveness moment that needs to take place first (a part of deconstruction). It is also possible that we need help with this from colleagues. As I write now, I am distinctly remembering a pupil who slapped me. Due to their change in home circumstances and the COVID-19 lockdown, the restoration piece is yet to happen a few months on – not ideal. I can feel the bitter taste around this, as we have not reconstructed how we will work together in the future yet. Despite huge global events out of our control and my empathy towards the child's very challenging homelife, it turns out I'm human too. We still need a conversation that addresses some of our more challenging times together, as well as the positive ones, that then helps us *both* work out how we move forwards in a positive manner.

OPPORTUNITY FOR OWN CREATION

We don't always learn new skills on the first teaching – as the snowboarding instructor who I worked with in Bulgaria can attest to; despite his detailed physics-focused instructions, I didn't manage to stand up on my own once – in a three-hour session. He despaired. I'm not sure I'll snowboard again. We need opportunities to try new learning, and even if we understand it intellectually doing it is another thing. (I don't get to go up many snowy mountains.) We need opportunities to try and fail.

The advantage to approaching and viewing positive behaviour as a teaching point is that we can explicitly refer to it later. In my drama lessons, once we had explored *Be my friend, be my enemy*, I could refer to it in other lessons. This is particularly useful for Autistic pupils who often find abstract concepts and metaphor challenging to grasp. Referring to previous experiences and, for some pupils, visual aids, can mean the actions are easier to follow: "Remember how you asked Ms King if you could have glitter last lesson? She said yes? How can you ask in a similar way for the football at break?"

Schoolwide, if a particular pupil or class has been receiving teaching around positive behaviour it is useful to communicate this with colleagues: "Oh, I heard you did some really mature negotiation with Frank the other day, Mr Singh told me. Think we'll need those skills of yours again here if you want to negotiate a homework deal." Highlighting situations as another opportunity for pupils to use their new skills can work wonders – it gives them an opportunity to succeed. Most of us want that.

POSITIVE FEEDBACK – WHAT WE APPRECIATE APPRECIATES

What we appreciate appreciates, i.e. what we concentrate on grows (Twist, 2014). Positive feedback is vital.

The day I learnt the most about teaching was the student observation day during my PGCE. Simply, we were to follow a pupil for a six-period day, from class to class. The class knew I was a trainee observing, but they didn't know the specific pupil I was observing. My professional tutor had chosen the pupils 'known for their behaviour'. The boy I had was challenging for most of his teachers; I learnt why – nearly everything that he heard from an adult during the day was negative; "You're late, take your coat off, where's your homework? Stop talking. Stop doing that. Why are you doing this? Why haven't you done that?" I do not blame the teachers for this. In each of their fifty-minute sessions they had objectives and content to get through, however the accumulative effect of only receiving negativity was evident: it didn't make him feel good, he reacted negatively. How do you feel on those days that the world seems to be against you? You argue with your partner, the bus driver is rude, the receptionist grunts at you and a pupil tells you to f*** off – it can affect us, and it affects our pupils.

Now, I am not suggesting we lie or transform into Disney characters (unless that's your teaching style), but find the small moment of positive affirmation. An old teacher of mine once said to me that the best behaviour management strategy to get respect is to ask someone to do something for you and then praise them for it: "Jahed, could you pull that blind down for us please? Great, thanks for that." The child has been recognised for something positive – and it's genuine. *This* can be built upon.

Positive feedback *is* one of the magic silver bullets for improving behaviour. For pupils who are not used to it, especially ones who are usually labelled 'the naughty kids', a piece of positive feedback can be a game changer. Some practical ideas of how to do this:

PHONE CALLS HOME

When working full time I have a quota of three calls every week. It is the last thing I do on a Friday afternoon – ring three homes and say something positive about their children. Parents and carers have been pleasantly surprised to receive such calls and it's a great appreciation exercise to finish your week on. (Pro-rata for part-time/ flexi-hours. If you're job sharing, ensure this task is shared as it will strengthen the relationships with pupils moving forwards.)

POSITIVE POSTCARDS HOME

Paul Dix (2017) advocates to send a positive postcard home when a pupil does something positive. Whilst they may nonchalantly take your bit of paper and shove it into the bottom of their bag, alongside the yoghurt pot and used condoms wrappers, this physical manifestation of positivity can be a treasured piece. For some pupils it may be hard to find something to give them one for, or it wouldn't be fair compared to what you are giving them out for with other pupils. In this case Paul suggests tearing it into four – explicitly explaining to a pupil that you want to give them a positive postcard, and they can earn it by quarters (Dix, 2017). This is a form of scaffolding – we would do it in the academic work, we can do it here (also, nice to give them a fresh complete one when they're done rather than four grubby bits sellotaped together).

COMPLIMENTS

They do need to take their coat off in the classroom, there's some school policy about it, but how about you compliment it first: "That looks like a snuggly coat, I need something like that myself, really nice. OK, time to pop it off though, we're three minutes in, you know the rules" is much more likely to get you positive results rather than shouting "Why is your coat on in the classroom? Take it off immediately!"

It is worth warning around compliments, however, to be very sensitive to the pupil and their own self-image and confidence. It's much safer to compliment things and actions as opposed to appearance – it can get you in sticky water and is best avoided. This includes haircuts. Unless pupils specifically bring it up themselves as a topic they are happy to talk about, it can be a sensitive area, particularly for children in care. For these children it is often a Social Worker who has the authority to make decisions about haircuts, similarly in a separated family unfortunately haircuts are sometimes used as a bargaining tool between adults who are not getting on or agreeing – so best to stick to pencil cases, handwriting, acts of kindness and so on.

EXPLICIT RECOGNITION

Sometimes, just verbalising positive behaviour is enough; "Joe, you've got your pen ready, excellent, you're ready for the title, it's on the board" has a far more positive, learning focused tone than "Joe why haven't you written the title yet? Laura is on question two already." Keep the focus on the learning, and explicitly describe how they can get to the next stage – again, this is scaffolding, we do it in academic work.

Let us look at a scenario:

You see Luke, he has forgotten his book (again) and he's texting on his phone.

Option 1: From your desk you see Luke's lack of work and project across the classroom: "Luke, I can't believe you've forgotten your book again, this is terrible, that's five more behaviour points, five more and I have to call home. What and you're on your phone? You know the rules. OK so that is five more behaviour points, I will be calling home at lunchtime. Now get some paper and try and catch up if you can."

What message does Luke get here? He has failed (again), he is terrible, he now has to worry about home's reaction, he was actually texting his Dad to ask if he could bring in his PE kit that he's forgotten, as he knows he will get in trouble for that too. The teacher has said "try and catch up if you can" which tells Luke that the teacher doesn't believe that he can do this, why bother if he's going to fail again anyway? Easier to scroll through TikTok under the desk. All the other pupils have heard the altercation, they can see that Luke is defying your rules, and so are there really any rules? Maybe they can pretend to have forgotten their book and browse TikTok too?

Option 2: You see Luke's lack of work. You are helping someone else, so for now you look over, make eye contact so that he knows that you have seen him. You don't say anything at this stage, the look may be enough. Unfortunately it isn't, so at the next available moment, you go to him, crouch down and quietly speak with him.

You: "Luke, can't help noticing you're not on task, what's going on?"

Luke: "Forgot my book, can't work."

You: "Oh dear, that's not the first time is it, do you know where your book is?"

Luke: "Yes, in my bedroom. Just forgot it."

You: "OK, how can I help you remember for next time? You know forgotten equipment is behaviour points, it will be really annoying if you keep adding those up just for forgotten equipment."

Luke: "Yeah. I just forget."

You: "OK, well I can see you have your phone out already. Obviously that will be going in your bag very soon or in my desk drawer. But whilst it's out how about I help you set a reminder for next Thursday morning before our lesson to remember your book?"

Luke: "Yeah, alright" (does so, possibly with your help).

You: "Great, so back to today, can you resist temptation if your phone's in your bag or does it need to be in my desk?"

Luke: "My bag's fine."

You: "OK, your decision – just to remind you, you know the consequences if I do see it out again, and I will be checking."

Luke: (Grunts.)

You: "So, did you get what we're doing now? I've grabbed some paper for you anyway so you can get on, the title's on the board, that first question about hydraulics, do you remember what that's about?"

You proceed to 'talk' the answer to the first question together, Luke may need a sentence starter or a few key vocabulary words to answer the question, which you can write or help him write on his paper.

"Great, you're all on task, you get going with question one then. I'll check in with you in a bit, look forward to reading your answer."

After a while you return to Luke, he has at least had a go at question one. This gives you opportunity to praise his efforts, correct any misunderstandings and guide him onto the next question.

At the end of the lesson you have a quick word with Luke, reminding him about expectations for next lesson. "So Luke, with that reminder on next lesson it will be great to see your book again and not have to keep adding on these behaviour points. I'll keep the work you've done today and we can stick it in so your good work is not lost! See you Thursday."

What message does Luke get here? You're on it, he can't get away with phones and forgotten books in your lesson, but you have helped him with this – showing that you care. This increases Luke's respect towards you. Not many (if any) other pupils heard the conversation, you did not set up a narrative within the classroom of 'Luke is the one who fails' in front of others, so Luke doesn't have to consider peer reactions or his reputation. You took the time to help him, and even though he is far behind his peers, rather than pointing that out you just helped him get back on the path. You gave Luke subtle scaffolding that makes him feel he *can* achieve the task, therefore there is more of a reason for him to have a go at it. He understands that you will still be keeping an eye out for the phone and you have reminded him of the consequences – Luke has heard these boundaries and expectation reminders but does not feel threatened or on alert. When you return to him, it shows that you are an adult who keeps their word, he respects you for this. The reminder at the end of the lesson once again shows that you care, but you are holding a high expectation for him. Very few others were aware of the conversation, and even those nearby only heard you upholding expectations and explicitly recognising a re-focus on the learning. Others will subconsciously know that they will most likely be treated in a similar way and that your lessons have a strong focus on learning.

DISPLAY AND USE MODEL EXAMPLES

I once spent a long afternoon photographing the best part of every pupil's mock exam essay in a mixed ability GCSE group. Granted, it took a while, but the effect was miraculous and lasted several weeks. I embedded them within a PowerPoint presentation, circling the parts that would 'get them the points' for the exam. Often model examples are from our high ability (more often 'well behaved') pupils. In the easier questions where the lower ability pupils could do well, I used their work instead. The lower ability pupils in the group didn't even bother to look at the board at first when I said "here are some model examples I found in your work" – it was never *their* work that got chosen for this. Only, it was this time. Importantly, I didn't name names. All the work was anonymous. When Mike, a low ability pupil 'known for his behaviour' saw his work on the board his whole persona changed. He looked, looked away, went bright red, became very still, looked again – he couldn't believe it. I didn't have to say anything, I continued to anonymously use his work as a teaching point ("so what's great here is that this pupil has laid their argument out clearly at the start, signposting the reader with 'I do not believe this statement to be true'"), I was able to praise him without making a fuss about *him*, his work had become exemplary. He worked hard for the rest of the lesson. This had a similar effect on a couple more of the more easily distracted pupils – through using their good work as the focus *not* their negative behaviour, their distracting behaviour disappeared. (See Further Reading AQA DIRT lesson, can be easily adapted for your pupils.)

A final note on positive feedback: for some pupils it will (initially) be too much. If they're not accustomed to it they may think you're being ingenuine or making fun of them. You may receive abuse, your positive postcard ripped up or *The Blank* – continue regardless. Be consistent with your kindness. The defensive response is a protection mechanism, they don't know how to handle praise because their inner story is that they don't deserve it. I dare you to be the teacher who showers them with positive feedback at every opportunity anyway and break the cycle.

SELF-REGULATION

Self-regulation is widely discussed in Alternative Provisions, Special Schools and PRUs and is an approach that I advocate in mainstream schools. A small under-standing of stress, how it affects our behaviour, and how to manage it can be of huge benefit for both ourselves and our pupils. Luckily, there are many people talking about it now. Stuart Shanker, who helped develop The Mehrit Centre in Canada, has developed a useful framework and resources to help educators with this. They state:

> The original psychophysiological definition of self-regulation refers to how we respond to stress – whether in a manner that promotes or restricts growth. Mindful self-regulation, which enhances learning and emotional, social and physical well-being, involves learning to recognize and respond to stress in all its many facets: positive as well as negative, hidden as well as overt, minor as well as traumatic or toxic. (Shanker, n.d.)

If a pupil is stressed, for whatever reason, and they respond to it with an outwards negative action they will continue to restrict their ability for growth. If, on top of that, we respond in a negative way – shout, immediately punish, shame – then we are restricting the young person's growth further. Sometimes this might be necessary – the child is about to drill through their hand (or through someone else's hand – I was almost a witness to this) – they may require a further burst of stress to protect them, to ignite the fight, flight or freeze response. Most of the time, however, this is not necessary. Shanker defines stress as "Anything that requires our internal system to burn energy in order to maintain balance". (Shanker, n.d.). So clearly, if a pupil is stressed the body's system is sending the energy towards maintaining a balance – not concentrating on your introduction to oxbow lakes.

Outwardly we witness the 'bad behaviour'; if we can recognise this to be an indi-cator of stress then we can help regulate it: "recognise the difference between stress behaviour and misbehaviour" (Shanker, n.d.). We can start this recognition process in ourselves, what are those idiosyncratic, seemingly involuntary negative actions that happen when we're stressed? Biting nails? Snapping at others? Tappy foot? – and then how does this escalate and when would we recognise it as stress? – as we grab the phone to mindlessly scroll? The cigarette? The wine? Or when we've had days of not being able to sleep, not eating and unknowingly become dangerous as we drive? What makes this recognition game more fun is that we all have different signs for stress; one pupil may chat, another may put their head down and sleep in your lesson – we return to the importance of building relationships with our pupils. Only by knowing our pupils over time will we be able to spot the signs earlier – and there-fore help them. Shanker offers a comprehensive framework for supporting self-regulation for young people:

1. **Reframe the behaviour:** "Becoming mindful of the kind of assumptions and biases we have that cloud our perceptions or skew our perception of why children or teens behave the way they do."
2. **Identify the stressors** across the five domains of stress: physical/biological, emotional, cognitive, social and prosocial
3. **Reduce stress:** in the moment apply strategies that relieve the stress
4. **Reflect:** enhance stress awareness. "Have opportunities to learn how it feels to be truly calm."
5. **Respond:** "Develop personalised strategies to promote resilience and restoration." (Shanker, n.d.)

Once we have reframed the behaviour, given the situation space to consider that this behaviour may be more than the surface struggle, we can get curious. A child hits another; it's not the first time. We are likely to assume, from past experience, that a similar pattern is playing out, that the child who hit is to blame and needs punishing. Whilst this still might be the case, let's consider why: when do humans hit other humans? When they feel scared, stressed, overwhelmed – we have identified a stressor. In the moment we need to reduce that stress – we separate the pupils, maybe we take the perpetrator to a calm space away from the class and provide sensory experiences that reduce stress in that moment (blankets, a walk outside, breathing exercises etc.). Before we have done this, there is no point dissecting the scenario – the pupil is in hyperarousal (see Chapter 4), they will be unable to 'hear' you. Once in a regulated state, it's time to reflect – this may even be later in the day. As the framework suggests, this is an opportunity to learn how it feels to be calm – we can start here – "How do you feel now? How is that different to when you hit your friend?" Finally, respond: a pupil who is unable to manage their stress needs help – from an experienced adult. They need to be taught and learn how to respond better next time. This is the personalised section – you can develop a plan. This will come from questioning – "when did you first start feeling angry? How did that feel in your body? What was your mind doing? What can we put in place here that will help you to stay calm?" Often the answer involves breaking the cycle and interrupting a negative stress load with an alternative sensory experience. Sometimes the pupil has already attempted to do this themselves (usually unconsciously), however unfortunately, that still may well look like disruptive behaviour – they can feel themselves getting frustrated with work they can't do, so they get up, walk around and start chatting to a friend – their system is telling them to get away. In a more serious example, some young people who struggle to manage their own energies, anger and emotions will self-medicate, often with weed or self-harm; their bodies crave the release from the pressure that's building up. It is an unfortunate circumstance that their own unconscious attempts at self-regulation will also be punished – and so no progress is made. Instead if we, as educators, can provide safe (and legal) methods of self-regulation, we can give pupils a tool for life – that may well keep them out of trouble and danger in the future. Old pupils of mine have returned to me years later telling me "Miss, I still do that breathing thing you taught us when I'm stressed." Wow.

A fantastic resource for ideas on activities and exercises to help self-regulation at each stage is provided by Family Action. Some councils provide countywide training in all of their schools (see Further Reading).

Interview

It's not just about thinking you feel safe in order to be good at learning, it's about feeling safe on a nervous system level. Feeling safe from threats both perceived and real – and that's what self-regulation is.

Kate McAllister is a qualified teacher with more than ten years' experience in leadership and management roles. She is an associate at the UCL Institute of Education in London and co-founder of www.rethinking-ed.org where she works with school leaders and teachers on developing effective practice. She is co-author of *Fear Is The Mind Killer* (Mannion and McAllister, 2020) which tells the story of implementing a highly effective Learning Skills curriculum in a UK secondary school. After working in the Calais refugee camp known as 'The Jungle', she also co-founded The Human Hive, which brings high quality, inclusive learning experiences to people who cannot access formal education. The first permanent Hive School is now open in the Dominican Republic.

 In terms of facilitating self-regulation with pupils, Kate says she stumbled upon it initially through school trips; she discovered that when she took the more 'challenging' pupils out on trips rather than the expected 'fish out of water' reaction she was expecting, she discovered a sense of "group, safety and camaraderie" which she then tried to replicate with as many trips as possible,

> because in that space they seemed more open to learning. What I was trying to do was move away from the dragging defiant horses to water style of teaching and to make them want to go to the learning. That got me thinking about what is it about being in a classroom that makes them feel so resistant to learning? Maybe it has something to do with feeling more valuable in the classroom than outside of it? If that's the case, then why doesn't it feel safe in the classroom, when objectively it is safer? The outside world can't get in, the rules of engagement are fairly set, so what is it about that that seems to have a counter effect? That's when I started thinking about where they felt welcome, where they felt safe and finding out what they needed. I thought it was a necessary requirement in order to be able to teach them, but I didn't realise how vital it was on a fundamental neurobiological level.

Kate goes on to explain these neurobiological impacts that can distract our pupils from learning:

> We have a nervous system that's evolved with us since the beginning. It's evolved to keep us safe; it's a defence system. So if there's any perceived threat in our environment or on our mental dashboard that we're carrying with us from home, it impacts on our ability to regulate all our internal

(Continued)

workings. Our heart beat remains slightly raised, our pupils are dilated, our hearing is different, we are hypervigilant because we are primed for the threat that we feel is coming. All of that takes away from our pre-frontal cortex, reduces our bandwidth for doing the more human stuff like connecting with other people, making jokes, writing poetry, concentrating on MFL lessons and so on.

In describing how Kate used this knowledge to help the pupils' ability to learn, she says:

First I regulated the safety of my environment. I calmed things down in the room, got rid of the chaos, tried to make my environment more safe and welcoming to others. I had noticed, if you change the environmental factors, pupils often behave differently. That was my first step. But it wasn't really about objective safety. There's a rationale that if you set the conditions for safety and they are objectively safe, everybody will feel safe inside them and therefore they will make better choices. You can see the rationale, but that's not quite how it works. People inside that space who have a dysregulated nervous system will still feel unsafe, so they will still act out, because the safety is still not radiating from within them outside. So self-regulation is about understanding what makes us feel and behave as we do and being able to change our internal sense of safety by ourselves.

I'm not sure that we're aware that we radiate vibrations around us. Many of us will recognise the child that you kind of dread them coming to your class because they are powerful, they have a powerful energy and you know that if they come in a bad mood they're going to affect the whole room. Or you have a sunbeam child, and when that sunbeam child is with a group everything just seems to go well. Atmospheres don't exist on their own, they are created by people. So as teachers if we can radiate an atmosphere of calm then our students will likely feel safer to be with us. That in turn has a calming effect on their nervous system; and that's co-regulation, you're sending messages backwards and forwards that it's safe to be with one another on a biological level. We back that up with our tone of voice and body language and everything else, which makes the teacher a very powerful person in the room. Often our first instinct is to 'manage' the behaviour of a potential threat to the calm atmosphere in a classroom. We raise our voices, become controlling and our nervous systems activate – as if we are preparing to fight an enemy. This can activate everyone else's nervous system too and the atmosphere can change very fast. But if everything about you says 'there's no threat here' – everyone else's nervous system in the classroom knows 'there's no threat for us here too.' If the majority of the class are able to remain calm, then they also have a co-regulating effect on the child who is struggling to regulate themselves. Our vibrations are contagious. Teachers can act as thermostats as well as thermometers.

Some simple strategies to self-regulate – for teachers who are not feeling calm too, Kate points out:

it's often intuitive, we take a deep breath or we go for a walk because it gives us that sense of spaciousness. These are self-regulating, but in a classroom environment children don't always have that freedom. So, when we say we want them to self-regulate, we don't always really mean it. Often what we want them to do is sit down and shut up so we can talk to them. What's lovely is when a room full of self-regulated children are wanting to do what you want them to do, but that doesn't always happen. Sometimes a child who is self-regulating needs to sit by themselves in the corner and just listen for a while without joining in. Sometimes a child who needs to self-regulate needs to take themselves for a walk and come back when they're calmer.

There are things teachers can do. It begins with understanding that we have a nervous system and it does all this stuff by itself; breathes in and out for us, makes our blood pressure goes up and down automatically – we don't have to tell it to, and wired into all those same systems is our defence mechanisms, which bypasses the pre-frontal cortex we will react to a potential threat without consciously thinking reflexively but we can go into manual override by noticing things like our breathing – for example when was the last time you heard yourself exhale fully? We tend to breathe in a very shallow way when our nervous system is activated so not being able to hear yourself exhale is a warning sign that we could do with down-regulating our nervous systems a touch. Or we can stretch our arms out, which makes us take a breath, and also tells our nervous system to cease and desist, there's no predators in the room.

Self-regulation isn't a thing you can learn overnight by doing a course, or reading a book, it's a practice. You start with a couple of bits, you add a few more bits and get better at it.

Source: Interview with author, 2020

Action Box

Next lesson

Find at least five opportunities to explicitly recognise positive behaviour. Keep this in the style of you and your teaching and find moments to thank or praise to highlight the action. E.g. – "could you hold these books a second? Great help, thanks." If you can link them to the next stage of learning even better – "Fin, you've got your book out already, you know what to do next."

(Continued)

Next week

Make three positive phone calls home. Reflect on your week and choose three pupils that you caught doing well in a way that was above *their* usual – whether with behaviour or work. So you might call one for an amazing three page essay that's going into the school competition, one for asking their first question in a group discussion and one for remembering all of their equipment for the first time (in week nine). What you appreciate appreciates.

Long term

Choose one to two pupils who challenge you the most.

1. Spend some time reflecting for yourself – what behaviour are they displaying? Where is the stress coming from? How could it be avoided? – sometimes it's as simple as a five–minute walk around the block in your double period.
2. Spend some time with the pupil – when calm – discussing what makes them stressed, find out how aware they are of their own process, body and reaction. Also find out what makes them feel calm. (Use the Family Action resource for ideas.)
3. With the pupil, devise a simple (three to five steps) plan to help them self-regulate. Share examples of when you or other adults do this too – allow them to know there's nothing wrong with them, it's just part of being human. Set a time to reflect and re-evaluate the plan and actually do it.

What has any of this got to do with behaviour?

Behaviour is contextual and learnt, therefore, if we want our pupils to behave in certain ways in order to be accepted in our classrooms, societies or cultures, we have to explicitly teach it. For those pupils who struggle to regulate their behaviour we must create opportunities for physical and emotional self-regulation. Punishing a pupils' lack of self-regulation will get us nowhere and can have damaging long term effects on the pupil.

Further reading

School Suspensions Are an Adult Behaviour – Dr Rosemarie Allen

A brilliant TEDx talk about how we are getting it wrong when it comes to our approaches to behaviour in schools, and how we can better help the pupils. Available from www.rosemarieallen.com/videos-.html (accessed March 26, 2021).

Fear Is the Mind Killer: Why Learning to Learn Deserves Lesson Time and How to Make it Work for Your Pupils – Dr James Mannion and Kate McAllister (2020)

James and Kate spent eight years working in schools on a learning curriculum. They discovered that teaching learning skills led to academic improvement for disadvantaged pupils. This book takes you through their process, "On the other side of fear is the teacher you want to be, and the children you'd like to teach."

Toolkit for Regulation: Maintaining Positive Behaviours in the Classroom – Lincolnshire BOSS Family Action

A practical toolkit of physical activities and games suitable for the classroom that help regulate pupils.

Key Stage 1&2: www.family-action.org.uk/content/uploads/2020/07/Toolkit-for-Regulation.pdf

Secondary School: www.family-action.org.uk/content/uploads/2020/11/Toolkit-for-Regulation-Secondary-Schools.pdf (accessed March 26, 2021).

The Mehrit Centre – Stuart Shanker

This website provides many useful videos and resources on self-regulation and how to support our young people. https://self-reg.ca/ (accessed March 26, 2021).

AQA English Language Paper 2 – DIRT lesson with marking codes – Adele Bates

Originally created for AQA English Language Paper 2, lesson exemplifying how to integrate pupil's model answers using DIRT (Dedicated Improvement and Reflection Time). https://adelebateseducation.co.uk/product/aqa-english-language-paper-2-dirt-lesson-with-marking-codes/

6

"MISS, YOU ARE THE WORST TEACHER EVER": DON'T TAKE IT PERSONALLY

#INSULTOFTHEWEEK

Pupil – Whilst defiantly stropping off into the corner of the room:

"Miss, I don't need YOU anymore, I have a DICTIONARY now!"

(She went on to do her first piece of independent extended writing.)

IN THIS CHAPTER YOU WILL

- Learn why attitudes from pupils that feel personal most often aren't.
- Discover how to respond to and look after yourself when you feel personally triggered by pupils.

INTRODUCTION

Don't take it personally.

Easier said than done.

I was working at an SEMH school one average morning, I entered the building as usual to prepare. The pupils arrived in dribs and drabs over the following half hour. Out of the eight pupils I said good morning to *every single one of them* told me to f*** off – before the 9am register. I was having a wobbly day, so I took myself to my teaching space, feeling a little fragile. Some of these pupils were ones I thought I'd built up a good relationship with. What had gone wrong? Was I being too keen? Too patronising? Too interested? Too much? Why were they being like that to me now?

Luckily, I caught this negative train to self-pity.

Experience has taught me that it's a fruitless journey, and whilst I still occasionally slip into it (what with being a human and all), in general I can catch myself – and if not, I have some trusted colleagues who can snap me out of it (see Chapter 8).

The reason *I know* that this doesn't work is because the focus is all wrong. I hate to be the bearer of shocking news, but a lot of the time teenagers don't actually give a shit about you and your insecurities. That is not to say, of course, that your relationship with them can't have a huge effect on them, their education and wellbeing, for better or worse, it's just that teenagers' brains are *wired* to put themselves first.

In one way this news can be devastating; that lesson you spent the entire weekend planning and got your mum around to help make individual Viking helmets for all your pupils with their names in genuine Viking alphabet? – Becky just started going out with Jo who has only just broken up with Sadia, so they're all wound up, not in the mood for role play, and just want to do something 'less cringe' – they don't give a shit how you feel about your Viking helmets. If you are an early career teacher being told repeatedly the importance of your job, the responsibilities you now hold and how you can shape your pupils' future lives ... it can feel daunting and on observation days, terrifying.

As a fabulous peer of mine observed during my own PGCE year about our lessons: "No puppies are actually going to die."

Remember, we are all learning *something* always – it's just it might not be the National Curriculum Syllabus, which is OK, because that's *not* the recipe for a fulfilling life.

There is clearly a balance to be had here. Yes, we need to care. My charismatic fellow Associate at Independent Thinking, Hywel Roberts, captures the essence of this well in his work around *Botheredness*: "At the heart of the world's best teaching you'll find one admittedly made-up word – botheredness." He links this to positive teacher acts: "smiling, laughter, encouragement, praise, time" (Roberts, 2012: 15). *And* there is a balance that still enables you to do your job, so that you don't become 24-hour obsessed with every move and murmur your pupils make.

To begin with, let's take a look at what we know (and this field is always expanding) about teenage brains.

TEENAGE BRAINS

we view infants' not being able to walk or talk as normal, but view adolescents' making a bad choice in the heat of the moment as a brain defect. (Casey, 2013: 80)

Adolescence is a time of biological changes in the brain that affect behaviour. Scientists and Psychologists now know that at this time the changes are unique in themselves; they are not merely a bigger version of the child brain or smaller version of the adult one. Acknowledged in the right way, adults can support teens in forming tools of resilience and awareness that equip them well into adulthood. However, if we don't understand these changes, belittle this key developmental stage or take to heart seemingly negative or reactive responses we can end up pushing away and unintentionally suppressing some of the most wonderful gifts that this stage has to offer.

One of the main functions of the adolescent brain is to prepare us to live independently from our primary caregivers, so that we might survive it alone; most mammals go through a similar developmental brain phase. The process begins from the back of the brain – the brain stem, to the limbic area and lastly to the pre-frontal cortex. It is the pre-frontal cortex that is in charge of evaluating, planning and reflecting – hence why teenagers often have a reputation for heightened risk taking – the very part of the brain that assesses risk is not fully developed. Unfortunately, this leads to the statistic that "unintentional injuries are the leading cause of death and disability among adolescents", many associated with car injuries (WHO, 2021).

Dr Dan Siegel, a clinical professor of psychiatry, teacher of mental health and father of two young adults explains that there are two main processes taking place in the brain at adolescence: Pruning and Myelin formation (Siegel, 2014b). Up until this point, the child's brain has been absorbing as much information as it can about the world; the teenager brain starts selecting – Pruning. It selects the information most useful to it and goes through a more finely tuned process of creating an identity – in contrast to their primary caregivers. If, as their educators, we can remember this, we can build it into our lessons, creating healthy opportunities for self-exploration, for example creative activities, exploration of different identities and cultures. If we do not allow space for this in a positive way whether at home or school and quash any signs of individualism, we squish the process of adult-identity-making in the brain. An unfortunate effect of this may be that they choose to do it in a non-safe, secret way.

Alongside this, the brain is forming myelin. This is a protective sheath that allows neurons to communicate with each other in a more effective way, enabling increased linkage. Siegel advises teens that during this remodelling stage they aim towards an integrated brain by pruning what's not needed and increasing linkage. He recommends doing Mindsight exercises to increase mental health and wellbeing (Siegel, 2018).

Both Siegel and the researchers working with Casey are quick to bust some myths surrounding teenagers (Casey, 2013; Siegel, 2014a, 2014b):

MYTH 1: TEENS HAVE RAGING HORMONES AND JUST NEED TO GROW UP

There is no scientific evidence that hormones can 'rage.' Puberty (typical onset: between 8 and 14 years (NHS, 2018)) does happen at a similar time to adolescent brain development, but not at the same time, the teenage brain may not be fully formed until the age of 25 years (Paradigm, 2021). It is a disempowering myth that suggests that the phase of changed behaviour must be endured, when in reality there are many things we and the teens can do to support them to cope and even thrive during this time – and it does take time: biologically they are different from adults, so the phrase 'just grow up' is unhelpful and unrealistic (Siegel, 2014a).

MYTH 2: TEENS ARE CRAZY, LAZY AND OUT OF CONTROL

Teen's brains experience more intense emotions than adults', as the signals from the limbic area and brain stem are more influential than what's going on in the higher reasoning pre-frontal cortex. However, Casey and Caudle argue that "when no emotional information is present, not only do many adolescents perform as well as adults, some perform even better [....] the description of teens as 'all gasoline, no brakes, and no steering wheel' [Bell and McBride, 2010: 565] more accurately reflects their behaviour in heated situations than in cool, less immediate, and less emotional ones. In these cool situations, the teen appears to be capable of acting rationally and making optimal decisions" (Casey and Caudle, 2013: 83). This gives a big hint to the type of calm emotional environment and communication that is most conducive to teens' learning.

MYTH 3: ADOLESCENTS NEED TO PUSH AGAINST ADULTS

Whilst this is a time for young people to discover the world outside of the childhood home, it does not mean they will reject *all* adults; on the contrary, they are actively looking for new role models. Again, this is something we can support with mentors and buddying schemes. If we build this into our young people's education in a positive way, they are less likely to turn to it elsewhere – gangs and groomers prey on teens who are looking both for new communities and new identities. Another place we see this play out is at parent and carer evenings; when you learn that the keen pleasant young person in your classroom has only grunted at their parents for the last two years – at this point I feel it is our job to help the parents and carers understand that *they* don't need to take this personally (Siegel, 2014a).

In his book *Brainstorm: The Power and Purpose of the Teenage Brain*, Siegel (2016) advises adults that instead of slipping into and re-enforcing these myths and feeling helpless as we watch our children metamorphose before our eyes, that we nurture the *ESSENCE* of the teen brain. This would help to both empower them and ultimately to support and inspire the adults around them. Siegel describes *ESSENCE* as *Emotional Spark, Social Engagement, Novelty Seeking and Creative Exploration.* For each one he discusses the positive and negative aspects. These are listed below with my recommendations on how this knowledge can help you take things less personally and how you can differentiate your teaching more effectively for these unique brains.

ES – EMOTIONAL SPARK

- More stimulus from the body through the brain stem and limbic area, so teens are more emotional.
- To the teen brain neutral situations can look hostile – hence why your innocent 'can I help you?' can be met with being told to f*** off.
- Can experience negative emotions intensely and if not supported, teens can learn to suppress these emotions, live only in their pre-frontal cortex and lose the vitality of life.
- The increased amount of emotion evokes motion – to become more independent.
- Increased experience of fun and passion. (Siegel, 2016)

IN THE CLASSROOM

Teens can move swiftly between emotions: aggressive one minute, calm the next, back to annoyed. In the classroom we have a choice – we can go up and down with every emotion shift (times 30 odd in the class) or we can give them the space to feel into their own emotions. One teen Siegel interviewed gave us some helpful advice, for adults to leave teens more space to experience feelings that arise before rushing to get involved or trying to help (Siegel, 2018). Not every rolled eye or tut needs a punishment. Pick your battles and don't make a teens' reaction more of an issue than it needs to be – it will escalate, you will lose and more time is taken away from the learning.

DON'T TAKE IT PERSONALLY

The f*** off/huff/shrug/moan is most likely not personal. Neuroscientists have carried out experiments that show only 50% of teens can correctly identify emotions on photos of people's faces (Solihull Approach, 2013). The teen could be experiencing your neutral interaction as a threat to their safety and reacting accordingly – a reaction useful for keeping yourself safe when you first attempt to become independent from your main caregivers. This is not a conscious recognition. Knowing this shows us that the reaction is not personal. Yes, it may need to be dealt with (e.g. there are consequences for swearing), but with this understanding you can *respond* and educate rather than *react*.

SE – SOCIAL ENGAGEMENT

- Increased need for belonging and collaboration.
- Can fall into peer pressure: giving up morality to gain membership.
- Belonging to a community is proven to increase happiness, health in body and mind and lengthen life expectancy. (Siegel, 2016)

IN THE CLASSROOM

We can increase the sense of belonging within our classroom and schools (see Chapter 7) in a healthy and safe way. In larger schools, the use of houses or teams can be useful to ensure everyone feels they have a place. Activities and explicit learning around values and belonging are key – not just the school motto on the website that no pupil ever looks at.

DON'T TAKE IT PERSONALLY

This understanding demonstrates to us why sometimes a pupil – who you know is capable of a task – refuses to do so in class. It's not personal. The need to fit in with peers is increased, and most likely will be more important for the survival-interpreting part of the brain than getting another detention. We can account for this by being sensitive as to when and what we ask pupils to do in front of others. We can also use friendship groups and collaboration as a helpful tool in group work.

N – NOVELTY SEEKING

- Enables independence and secretes dopamine – that feels good.
- Teens can become easily bored and dismissive.
- The hyper rational thinking doesn't engage as easily, so they just might not give a shit.
- An increased amount of courage to try new things and form new ideas. (Siegel, 2016)

IN THE CLASSROOM

The more we can build in safe novelty seeking and new experiences the more likely the pupils are to be engaged in the learning – their dopamine makes it feel good. It doesn't have to be complicated; I once took a Year 9 English class outside to write poems – the response was as if they'd been on a rollercoaster – and their creative writing was taken to a whole new level that we could not have accessed sat in rows in the normal classroom.

DON'T TAKE IT PERSONALLY

In the eyes (or brain) of a teenager, you are boring. It is not *you* personally, but the perspective from which they see you. In one school, where I support literacy and work a lot in the library, I am known by many as 'Miss Boring who reads boring books' – and when they found out I knit too? It was a whole new level of boredom. Take it as engagement: whilst they are passing judgement on your lesson/dress sense/jokes, they are engaging with you. Being labelled as boring rarely stops you from being able to form a positive relationship with them. Some lessons will be boring to teenagers, that's OK and an important lesson for them to learn – spice it up when you can to retain engagement and motivation.

CE – CREATIVE EXPLORATION

- Pushing against the status quo.
- An expansive imagination as they experiment with the different paths of life they may choose.
- Teens can realise that their current situations are not good and experience sadness and frustration about it. (Siegel, 2016)

IN THE CLASSROOM

Creativity is key to healthy, integrated brain development. For some that may be paint, glitter and costumes, for others it's being set a problem puzzle to investigate with algebra. Often when the curriculum is so content heavy, the creative tasks are left to the end of a topic or as an extension task – meaning only a few pupils get the opportunity to be creative. This is a tragedy – it might be the ones who are slower with set tasks, who could benefit from or thrive with the creative tasks the most.

What happens if you turn your lesson upside down? Can the creative task be the starter that sparks the engagement? In the 21st century it feels there are many large issues we need to solve for the human race: poverty, climate change, inequality, violence, wars, pandemics, and so on. We need creative solutions for these – there will not be an a, b, c step guide to approaching them. Fostering creativity in a teen's brain not only helps the individual but helps us invest in young people who could well be solving some of our world's greatest troubles in a few years. We need to make space for them to think.

DON'T TAKE IT PERSONALLY

Teens will push against you, your instructions, your lessons, your choices – this is a healthy demonstration of their creative brain development. It's not personal. *But why do we have to do this?* – great question to receive, do you know yourself?

STILL NOT CONVINCED THINGS AREN'T SO PERSONAL?

Let us look at a real life example:

In one of my supply circuit days, I visited a large mainstream comprehensive secondary school. One lesson a pupil and I got on the wrong side of each other. He wouldn't put his phone away, I challenged him, he thought it would be great to see how far he could push the supply teacher. It got to the "let's step out and have a chat" stage, at which point an unfortunately unhelpful SLT member walked past. Feeling inadequate, my own insecurities pounding in my head, I tried to take the 'strict and example' route: it failed miserably. The pupil became irate, I lost my cool and then as the SLT approached I had to 'ask for help' as "I'm not used to this school yet" and "could you remind 'us' of the rules around phones please, Sir?" To add to my increasing sense of failure was my self-judgement that I – a young, female supply teacher – had had to fall back on asking for help from a 'man in management'. Unsurprisingly, the pupil agreed in front of the SLT then returned to class to continue as he had left off – on his phone.

I took this situation home and I took it personally. Even though I knew it wasn't a competition I knew he had won, he had got to me, found my Achilles heel and picked at it – as only a teenager knows how to do. His vendetta against me was clear and he had triumphed before a glowing audience all on his side – the other 32 class-mates – whilst I had failed as a teacher.

Luckily, it was supply and I was somewhere else the next day. The incident fell into my pile of 'like-to-be-forgotten', moments of teaching.

A few months later I was sent again to this school. Lots must have happened in the interim schools, as I had more or less forgotten about the incident and the pupil – it's not easy with supply to remember which child belongs to which school; that was until he swaggered into the science lesson I was covering.

Whilst taking the register I momentarily looked at him, as the battle (not-that-it-was-a-battle) came flooding back to me in full musical technicolour. "Yes Miss" he murmured – Compliant? No phone? He was luring me into a trap. My Spidey sense was on alert. I set the class to work with the always-quite-dull-supply-teacher-instructions then oh so casually did a circuit of the room that *happened* to end at the boy next to my ~~nemesis~~ acquaintance. I had to say something, I had to know where we would recommence the fight:

"Oh, haven't you been in one of my lessons before?"

"Yes Miss" And he paused.

I thought: "That was it? Did I need to remind him that he had momentarily succeeded in bringing my, then 16 years of, teaching experience and knowledge metaphorically to its knees?"

I managed to hold myself, to remember one of my *own* 'top tips for behaviour' – look for the positive, focus on the learning:

"I'm sure we'll get on better today. How are you getting on with the task?"

The young gentleman, a shining example of Boy Scout, the epitome of quintes-sential English politeness explained what he'd done so far. Not *one* inkling of sarcastic undertone. Flabbergasted and disbelieving I re-chanted my top tip to myself (look for the positive, focus on the learning).

"Looks like you know this topic well, I'm sure you'll be fine with this lesson then."

"Yes Miss, last time you saw me I was just in a bad mood."

I went to do what supply teachers do best: sat at the front of the room, behind my desk (science block equivalent where there's nowhere to put your knees) and watch children work in front of me: my insides confused and reeling. The whole incident *had not been personal.*

Interview

Remind yourself of why you're doing this – because you want to make a difference. You're not doing it because it's easy work, because it's a breeze. Enacting change is difficult.

Mark Goodwin has 20 years' experience as a teacher, school leader, trainer and coach. He is the founder of Equal Parts Education, a company that delivers a turnaround programme for permanently excluded students across the Midlands, as well as working in partnership with schools and universities to deliver training and coaching to staff at all stages of their careers. Mark's passion is still the classroom and he can be found most days teaching across all phases, in mainstream, alternative and special.

Mark believes that not taking things personally begins with the wellbeing of the adult:

The adult may need help in order to react in a different way. They may need help with their wellbeing; their emotional wellbeing, their emotional receptors, and so on. I'm very clear with NQTs, you can get your bum bitten by a kid if you're not on top of your game, and that can happen twenty years later.

Mark reflects,

It hurts more at different points of your career. The stinger for me early on was "this lesson's boring" – you've planned the lesson, do you know how long it took me to cut these cards? Or draw these out? Early on in your career you're doing all this and the kids are like "Meugh." Another stinger for me is always the money, when a kid says to you "you're only in this for the money", especially when you're in a meeting after school with them. With pastoral work, it's easier not to bother, not to give the time, so that stung.

Mark gives an honest reflection of what it actually feels like when things get personal, and importantly, what he does about it:

What gets me is if I think a kid doesn't like me. Everything I'm trying to do is building a relationship. That happened only recently, a girl I work with, she was not buying the Goodwin happy-clappy, I mean, absolute respect that she even came and sat with me, knowing the life that she'd had. But she could push a button. You try all these things that have worked, I was trying all my repair work and giving her time to reflect – and she'd just say, "no, I don't want to do that. I just want to copy." That to me is like anti-learning, I'd rather do a worksheet and a closed exercise where there's a little bit of thought. At that point it was stinging – but it was letting myself say, "that's fine". It was hard for me, it was anti-teaching – but it was what she needed at the time.

You have to work at that, because I do take it personally, but I've built my resilience around that. People who do this type of work, they need good people around them. When I was working with that girl, I used to finish the session broken, I wanted to go back to my car and cry, nothing was landing. This is where I used to pick up the phone and ring my colleague. You need someone who says "you need a conversation, I'm here to help you."

Mark continues on what he observes as he supports and coaches teachers now:

some teachers get so isolated; they're new teachers, their mentors or HOD don't care or can't care. That's where the good old fashioned colleague, moan and groan, huff and puff, let rip and we roll our sleeves up and go again is needed, but younger staff need to hear that it still stings. It's about professional resilience, they need to really look after themselves, so they can leave it at work, have a conversation with someone and come back the next day with a clean slate for the kid *and themselves.*

Back to the pupils, Mark shares a matrix he works with, that helps him to explain to teachers how nuance is important: support > < challenge.

The most helpful relationship for any kid, is that you need to be up on the challenge as well, you don't camp out in the support. What helps for me is the coaching methodology, you're a coach, you're holding up a mirror; the kids mean the world to me, but that's no help to me if I'm letting them off with not working. It's having the skill and conversations to help them do what they don't want to do; it's not just about giving the kids a cuddle and some nice easy colouring to do, but it works on the other way, you can't just shout at a kid and tell them to do the work.

Personally, I do this work because I want kids to be independent, I want kids not to need me, not to need a one-to-one or a teacher: remember it's about independence. So whilst you're enjoying the relationship remember that it's about independence, you've got to push the kids to make decisions for themselves. Be friendly but don't be their friend, it's about relationship management. At its worst, help can enfeeble a kid and make them dependent.

We finished the conversation where we started – with the importance of teachers supporting their own wellbeing first:

Wellbeing has become a far more open conversation. I started teaching in 1999 and didn't have a wellbeing conversation for the first five years of my career – partly because of my gender, partly because people perhaps thought I didn't need one – it was a different culture. It took me a long time to find out about it. It's a whole lot better now, and I think it's brilliant that

(Continued)

people have a chance to say "I'm struggling, it's hard, I don't get it" and there are loads of wonderful people out there who will help you, and there are some brilliant schools, but there are still too many who tell you to just roll your sleeves up.

Source: Interview with author, 2020

Action Box

Next lesson

Collect and share an #InsultOfTheWeek. Being able to share and laugh about some of the hilarious or heart wrenching insults directed towards us by our cherubs can be very helpful. It gives us perspective and helps us learn that it's not just us. Share with my community of Inspiring Educators by tagging me in @adelebatesZ – let me know you got to Chapter 6 of the book!

Next week

Watch a few of Dan Siegel's videos on the teenage brain (see Further Reading). Bring an aspect into your lessons that could support one of the ESSENCE qualities of teenagers' brains.

Long term

Choose one to three pupils who challenge you the most behaviourally. Spend some time finding out about them outside of your lessons. You could:

- Talk to other teachers
- Talk to past teachers
- Read their EHCP if they have one
- Read their reports
- Look at their data around behaviour and reward points
- Engage them in Free Writing (see Chapter 3)
- Observe them in other lessons

Getting a bigger picture of a pupil (or anyone) gives us a wider context from which to understand another.

What has any of this got to do with behaviour?

When we take things personally, we react. Our insides are hurt and we seek to defend ourselves; this will only escalate an already challenging behavioural situation. Finding the distance when we can enables us to help the unmet need of the pupil more objectively, de-escalate challenging behaviour quicker and return the focus to the learning.

Further reading

Oops! Helping Children Learn Accidentally – Hywel Roberts (2012)
    An entertaining and useful book that guides teachers on how to use engagement in lessons to support learning and the curriculum. Also look out for Hywel's forthcoming book entitled *Botheredness*.

Brainstorm: The Power and Purpose of the Teenager Brain – Daniel J. Siegel (2016)
    A brilliant, accessible exploration, 'An Inside-out Guide to the Emerging Adolescent Mind, Ages 12–24' that sheds light onto how teenage brain development affects behaviour and relationships – and what to do about it! Suitable for parents, carers, educators and teenagers themselves.

The Adolescent Brain and The Remodelling Brain: Pruning and Myelination – Daniel J. Siegel
Useful videos that explain key concepts in teenage brain development.
    www.youtube.com/watch?v=0O1u5OEc5eY and www.youtube.com/watch?v=jXnyM0ZuKNU (both accessed 26 March 2021).

7

"MISS, I'M TOO THICK TO BE IN THIS CLASS": INCLUSIVITY, BELONGING AND BIAS

#INSULTOFTHEWEEK

On the phone to a pupil who is now going into school part time during lockdown –

Me: "How is school?"

Pupil: "Great!"

Me: "That's good to hear! Why's that?"

Pupil: "Because you're not there."

IN THIS CHAPTER YOU WILL

- Understand how inclusivity and belonging can affect behaviour and academic progress.
- Discover where your own biases are and what to do about them.

INTRODUCTION

Think of a time you didn't feel included in a social situation.

You were the younger kid hanging out with the cool older kids. You feared being 'found out' and being told to stop playing with them. Or you spent some time with your partner's extended family. Whilst they were welcoming, it's just not your family and you're not sure if they're an elbows-on-the table kind of family. Perhaps you go to a conference with over 500 people, where you are the only visibly disabled educator – again. You're the only one who has to ask for chairs to be moved, to reserve a place where you can be physically comfortable. Everyone else can sit where they feel and mingle with who they want. Or remember your first day at a new job. Everyone knows each other, they know the IT systems, the banter and which one is Colin's mug, which is not worth touching.

Choose your situation and then gently put yourself back into that place. What did it feel like? What was your heart doing? What were your various limbs doing? Did you find something to distract yourself? Whereabouts in the room or space did you place yourself? What happened to your breathing? Your appetite? What was your mind doing? How were you talking?

Now imagine that you are asked to do a task that is outside of your comfort zone, one that you know you find difficult. Now imagine that you are asked to do this task openly in front of the very people you feel excluded by.

How does it feel?

Is it conducive to learning?

How easily will you retain the details of the task in your long-term memory?

Can you perform at your best?

To what extent are the emotions and thoughts of not belonging distracting you from the task?

Now take a few deep breaths. You're not there now; but perhaps you have come to the same conclusion as me: humans thrive when they feel they belong.

Permanent exclusion, temporary exclusion, internal exclusion, isolation – all of these words and actions separate pupils out; pull them out of the learning community of your school and send the message that they don't belong here. Yes, sometimes people need time away from others (most teachers would agree with that for themselves too). However, in your classroom if a pupil does not feel included or welcomed, why would they want to stay, conform and do your work?

"But of course I include everyone" we often reply. A quick scratch under the surface can reveal differently. *Every* time I have asked a trainee teacher to do a tally of who puts their hand up or speaks in class there is always a *huge* gender imbalance – boys are more likely to speak, girls are more likely to listen. What messages does this send? How inclusive are we being?

Nearly half (45 per cent) of LGBT pupils – including 64 per cent of trans pupils – are bullied for being LGBT in Britain's schools (Stonewall, 2018) – are any bullied pupils likely to put themselves forward to read a poem in your class? Black children are between four and six times more likely to be excluded than their white peers (Klein, 2000). Why? What are we getting wrong?

Belonging to the community is a very human desire, and if we feel safe, comfortable and positively recognised within our group we are more likely to take risks, try that difficult chemistry equation and excel – as we can lean on the sense of community – knowing that temporary failure of a task does not mean we are no longer accepted, or that there is something inherently wrong with us.

This chapter examines how we can build inclusivity and community, on a microscale within one classroom and schoolwide, to positively impact focus and learning.

BUT I TEACH CHEMISTRY… (GOING BEYOND PSHE)

Inclusion, belonging and bias are topics beyond PSHE. Thankfully, schools in the UK are moving past tokenistic, one-off-curriculum-down-days and assemblies in which we put minority characteristics on a pedestal. An increasing number of educators now acknowledge that unless pupils (and staff) feel included within the school community, they will not thrive. Belonging is inevitably intertwined with safety. Can you think of a time you felt physically, mentally, emotionally, spiritually safe but that you didn't belong? I struggle to. Your pupils cannot listen or learn about your chemistry equations if they feel they don't belong in your classroom. If safety and belonging are not present within me, my limbic stem is engaged, reacting to perceived danger. My pre-frontal cortex – required to learn and retain the new information you are teaching, is unavailable to me (see Chapter 6), I am more likely to be distracted, consciously or otherwise, looking for ways to regulate my nervous system; I tap my pen, I talk to my friend who makes me feel good, I talk over you so I can retain control and feel safer. You might recognise my actions as 'bad behaviour' and you may punish me as such, but you haven't got to the root of the issue; you don't include me, I don't feel safe, I can't learn.

Some examples on the impact of lack of inclusion:

- If I don't see role models I can identify with in your subject, how can I aspire?
- If my parents or carers don't speak the language of the school, how can they attend parents/carers evening or support my school life? (I can get away with more as they won't understand…)
- If I don't have a supportive or quiet environment to do my homework at home, and you don't provide me one at school, how will it get done? What will happen to me when I don't?
- If I have learning needs that are not accounted for, I can't access the learning. I will distract myself, others, and possibly give up.
- If I don't have somewhere safe to go to the toilet that aligns with my gender, I won't go at school. I will sit in your lesson in discomfort and pain.

- If school doesn't make me feel safe because of my difference, I am on alert. I cannot learn, my body is focused on surviving.
- If I only learn about humans that look like me, I may become scared, unsure or overtly against difference. This will affect who I choose to be friends with, partner with, work with and employ. I don't know it's OK to associate with Others.
- If I don't learn that difference is safe; that two or more people can live alongside one another with different sexual orientations, religions, views etc. happily, with no threat to one another. If I have learnt that the Other is a threat and I happen to have power, I may start a war – be that with my neighbour, a gang war on the streets or a technology war over nuclear bombs.

USEFUL TERMS

Some useful terms and ideas of how they may play out in your classroom:

BIAS AND UNCONSCIOUS BIAS

A bias is either to prefer or reject something based on your personal opinion or judgement. Our brains help us to store vast amounts of information by creating shortcuts. For example, tiger = danger, so get away. However, it also does this with people (and situations) that we are not familiar with. It does this to help protect us, but what it does is create a negative (or positive, with differing outward results) bias towards specific groups for no other reason than that our brain is trying to make a shortcut. Even if it were true once, it doesn't mean that it is in every situation; and yet if we are not aware of this bias, if we are unconscious of it, we will let it play out in the decisions we make. Personally, I have a bias towards the underdog, so in a classroom setting, if I don't check my bias, I may be neglecting the more willing and high ability pupils. I know this bias of mine, which helps me account for it and informs my practice. However, before I realised this, it was an *unconscious* bias. My *intention* wasn't to exclude anyone; however, the damage was still the same as if I had known and not readdressed the balance. Those lucky underdogs.

SYSTEMIC BIAS

Systemic bias is bias against certain groups built into an organisation or country's structure. For example, to train to be a teacher you need a certain amount of financial support and need to stop working elsewhere. This reduces the chances of single parents applying, or people who have been through the care system and do not have parental financial or living location support. There is no intention to discriminate specifically against these groups, however the system has been created without bearing them in mind, and the result is the same: there is a negative bias that means these groups would need extra support or help to access the same part of the system that the majority can access without barriers. In the long term, this means that fewer people from these groups apply, so they are less represented within an organisation, they are less likely to be in positions of power within an organisation or system, and so the cycle continues. They become the blindspot.

MINORITY

A group of people who are statistically a minority within a certain larger group. It is worth noting here that the term BAME, referring to Black and Minority Ethnic people, often used in the UK, is not completely accurate. Black and Brown people are in a global majority (Adebisi, 2019), however, it may be that within your school they are in a minority. A minority may also not refer to numbers; there are more women in the UK education workforce than men, however they sit as a minority in terms of their access to decision making, wages and positions of power. Context is everything.

DISCRIMINATION

Discrimination is unfair treatment due to someone's characteristics. Some of your pupils will experience this every day of their lives.

PRIVILEGE

> Privilege is largely invisible to those who benefit from it [...] providing one group with advantages denied to the other, advantages that are frequently unacknowledged by those who benefit from them. (McDermott, 2017: 28–29)

This was explained clearly by Peggy McIntosh in 1998 in her article in which she answered, in essence, the question: "What do I have that I did not earn?" I will have a go, play along:

I had a free childhood education. Someone (my Mum) taught me how to read and write. I can walk down most streets alone in my country knowing it is unlikely I will be attacked, however my gender suggests I am still more likely to be attacked than others (see below for more on this). If someone wrongs me by law I can go to the police, knowing that they will take me seriously. I can travel to most places in the world and know that someone will speak my language.

The walking down the street safely aspect changes if I am not on my own. If I am with my same-sex partner we may, and we have, been attacked verbally and physically in London in 2019. Of note, this is one of the few areas I am not in the majority (heterosexual), and thus my status in this instance of being a minority (bisexual, or 'appearing gay') takes away my privilege. To prove the point further, I was straight until I fell in love with my partner at the age of 27. So up until that point I had never thought twice about being with a partner, holding their hand or showing affection in the street – and was never attacked for doing so. It wasn't until that safety was taken away that I realised I had been privileged.

This rug being pulled from beneath me got me thinking, if that privilege exists that I didn't know I had until I lost it, what other privileges do I have that I can't see? In writing this chapter another one struck me: my colleagues who were children in care had no base from the age of 18. The state is legally responsible for them until then, and then they are classed as an adult. I, on the other hand, was able to go to university because I had not just some financial support, but I also had a home to return to every holiday that was rent free and came with free food. I still have that at (at the time of writing) the age of 36 if ever I needed it in an emergency. My friends whose childhood was spent in care do not have that. They are statistically less likely to get a degree. People without degrees are less likely to be in positions of power – even when that power would involve making decisions about themselves.

EMOTIONAL LABOUR

The extra emotional work that a minority must do in order to either access something a majority would not have to, or the extra emotional work they must do in order to continue to 'conform' to a society's culture. For example, when you teach *Dracula* in which all of the Gypsy, Roma, Traveller community are on Dracula's side and represented as 'the baddies', the pupil in your class who is from the GRT community has a decision – either they can speak up about the misrepresentation at the risk of you or their classmates not agreeing, and thus they discover that they are less welcomed in this space than they'd thought, because the majority believe the text to be an accurate depiction (it's on the GCSE syllabus that's stipulated by the government after all, and so are lots of other racist texts), *or* they can choose to stay quiet and internalise the questions, doubts and fear about their place of belonging within this classroom. Either way, it is left to the very person belonging to the minority to do the emotional work, and of course, whilst they're going through this, they're not taking in what you're saying about pathetic fallacy on page 57. In this scenario, the best thing the teacher can do is to address the depiction, and discuss why the author may have done it, when it was written, how that character may be represented now and so on. That way, the pupil *may* decide to contribute to the discussion from their perspective but is not expected to carry additional emotional labour. The message of inclusion, and questioning historical literature norms, is carried by the teacher.

INTERSECTIONALITY

> All of us live complex lives that require a great deal of juggling for survival [...] What that means is that we are actually living at the intersections of overlapping systems of privilege and oppression. Failing to acknowledge this complexity, scholars of intersectionality argue, is failing to acknowledge reality. (Linda Carty and Chandra Talpade Mohanty, quoted in Coleman, 2019)

Carty and Mohanty's point in the classroom could look like this: there may be two physically disabled pupils in your class, Jude and Preeti. Let's say they have a similar impairment – hearing. We may think initially that how we differentiate for one will work for the other. However, Jude is from a white family in the UK with parents who understand his needs and have the financial means to support him. On the other hand, Prieei is EAL, British Asian. She is looked after by her grandparents who do not speak English – they don't fully understand the support that is available for Preeti's condition, and therefore she does not have the same level of equipment to help with her hearing as Jude does. In your classroom, you are cautious to show images of disabled people and talk about them, however, you have a blindspot in that all the role models and images are of white people. Which pupil feels more included in your classroom? Which one can access learning more easily?

MARGINALISED

People in a powerless position within society, who are not represented by decision makers. For example, in May 2019, 25/27 white men voted in new legislation to make abortion illegal in the state of Alabama, with the exception of a woman experiencing a serious threat to her life (Durkin and Benwell, 2019). This is the strictest abortion law in the US that directly affects' women, non-binary and trans people. Not one person from these minorities was represented in the decision making. The two other white men refused to vote.

SINGLE NARRATIVE

Only representing one minority's story, for example, in school talking about Paralympians as your only example of disabled people, or famous musicians as your only example of LGBTQ+ people.

MICROAGGRESSIONS

Small actions that may not have malicious intent but require the receiver to do extra emotional labour. For example, when you do a Mother's Day activity in your classroom before checking if all the pupils have a mother in their lives.

GETTING PAST TOKENISM

A note on those tokenary assemblies: Diversity day, Equalities Afternoon, Disability Awareness Assembly, Human Rights Week, LGBTQ+ Month are *not* bad activities when it comes to embracing inclusion, unless that's *all* you do. I once worked in a mainstream school that proudly displayed its Equality Policy on the front page of its website, and yet did not provide a prayer room for its Muslim students. It is the *culture* of the school that we must shift, which we will explore further.

In addition, one-off minority focused events in schools tend to perpetuate a single narrative and sycophantic approach "Wow, look what *these* disabled people can do, they're so brave and inspiring," or "Nelson Mandela is such an amazing man for black people, other black people can now know they have no limits." In the first instance regarding disabled people, this is a patronising approach that still leads from the perspective of majority or privilege; amidst the disabled community it is not a miracle that Deaf people are married (sometimes to hearing people) and have a (signed) discussion about which cheese to buy in the supermarket; it is only from an ableist perspective that this becomes anything of note. The assembly that then celebrates this in a well-meaning and yet misguided narrative of wonder has some damaging underlying tones that disabled people *shouldn't* be able to do these things, and that the bar of success within society is lower for them. The term to describe this is infantilisation that Disability Activist and a great colleague of mine, Elizabeth Wright explains in an article:

> Infantilising a disabled person means you are treating them like a child. It may not be intentional (though perhaps in some cases it is). It happens when you see or find out that the person you are interacting with has a disability of some kind. It is a form of ableism that is part of the social structures that we live in. (Wright, 2020)

She goes on to explain the different forms this can take, including when people will avoid speaking to a visibly disabled person directly, and instead address the able-bodied person beside them.

Another message this gives to our pupils is that disabled people are less capable than their able-bodied counterparts; and thus they would not be the best people to work with, hire or associate with. Both the pupils sitting in the assembly who are of the minority and who are not, receive distorted messages: that difference also collaborates with value in society. One is good, the other is bad.

Over to Nelson; undoubtedly he is a man who did some incredible things and succeeded through seemingly impossible resistance, which yes, can be very inspiring. However, it does not negate the society-wide and systemic racism that we know exists within every culture, our institutions and our schools. In May 2019 the Timpson Report for the Department of Education on school exclusions discovered that Black Caribbean pupils are nearly 1.7 times more likely to be excluded than white pupils. So when Nelson Mandela's achievements are celebrated, and black people are not seen or spoken of again in a positive light until next Black History Month, again we send distorted messages; we perpetuate the myth that racism is no longer a problem, that these things happened in *other* times and places. We give the permission to disassociate from the situation and advocate that in our society "we don't *see* colour" anymore, because all is equal – once again, sharing the narrative of the privileged majority, not backed up by racial hate crime statistics in the UK.

In addition, neither of these assemblies have dealt with intersectionality. Nobody, outside of television, is only one characteristic.

HOW DO WE INCLUDE?

Firstly, we have to be open. Our individual life experiences have not given us the monopoly on all experiences – which I discovered acutely when I left (only) one majority. As such, it is our jobs as educators to learn. To question, listen, believe and adapt. In my three-month Behaviour Training programme, I facilitate this model. There is one session that always stands out to participants more than any other – the Student Consultation. I ask the school to select around ten pupils to take part, and importantly they should be pupils who are *known* for their non-conforming behaviour. I then facilitate a carousel interview, I provide a framework of questions for the teachers to ask, who can ad lib as they see fit. The teachers have been prepped to listen and take notes. Importantly, the pupils do not have to ask the teachers anything. The pupils, in this scenario, are the experts. If questions arise through the conversation, they are part of the natural process – and the pupils have made that decision to want to know more, to engage – oh, to learn more! There is usually pizza involved too as a sweetener.

The results are astounding. These are the pupils whose reputation leans on them being 'the naughty ones' and in this consultation, the very staff who have given them detentions, had serious words and expelled them are asking for their advice and opinions. But that's not the astounding bit. The astounding bit is the pupils' responses. Often the pupils express the *importance* of 'teachers who care', boundaries, routines, high expectations and consequences. Why? Because as one regularly detentioned pupil put it "I know we push it sometimes, but if there were no rules or you didn't tell us off there'd be chaos. We don't want that, it would be dangerous." They wouldn't feel safe. During the consultation, pupils make many suggestions relevant to their setting around behaviour and *guaranteed* they will suggest some easily actionable ideas that the teachers will not have thought of, alongside some wacky Silicone Valley slides into class type ideas.

The next step is for the teachers to believe. Once the pupils have left, we do a quick debrief with the staff on their findings. I find this must be quite short as staff are often bamboozled by the experience, impressed by these young people's intelligence and willingness to contribute *appropriately* and need digestion time. Finally, the findings inform the rest of our behaviour training as we strategise how the teachers can implement the pupils' findings.

- Question
- Listen
- Believe
- Adapt

(Rinse and repeat.)

This example was around inclusion of a minority of pupils often classed as 'badly behaved'. The model could be easily adapted for other settings. In one school in England, as the lead on Equality and Diversity, I was once asked by a pupil if we could have an assembly on Islamophobia. This is not my area of expertise, neither is Islam. I set up an open meeting to pupils one lunchtime to discuss 'Islam at school' – it was open to all pupils, and in addition, I practiced positive discrimination and personally invited some of our Muslim pupils. Around ten pupils arrived, two of whom were non-Muslim and were there to learn more. This meeting made me cry. I was sat with Year 11 pupils who expressed that in their entire education they had *never once* been asked what it was like to be Muslim in a majority non-Muslim school. They discussed the dilemmas of pleasing both school's cultural expectations and home's very different cultural expectations. They talked about headscarves and uniform, they talked about the attitudes of other pupils and staff. They talked about bullying. They talked about Ramadan. This was also the meeting that I discovered they had never been offered anywhere to pray. Of course, the pupils didn't agree on everything, demonstrating that it's so important to not assume that because you've had the opinion of one person from a minority group you know everything. More than anything the pupils seemed relieved and enlivened for being asked.

- **Question** – I set up the meeting and had a few prompting questions to begin with.
- **Listen** – I took lots of notes and only asked clarifying questions.
- **Believe** – I ensured I did not question their experiences, particularly of staff's attitudes.
- **Adapt** – Within a week we had a prayer room at the school.

Rinse and repeat – this is a model I use regularly. It's also helpful to check in again with pupils to see if any positive (or negative) changes have occurred.

FINDING BLINDSPOTS AND GETTING IT WRONG

You have to be ready to feel uncomfortable.

During the editing process of this chapter, I was pulled up on whether the term 'blindspot' was appropriate when discussing discrimination. That felt icky, I'm writing on the topic, it didn't feel good to have got it wrong! I researched, asked questions of people who knew more than me and learnt. (The general consensus from Disability Activists and writers is that it is a spot that is not being sighted, rather than a perojative term towards a person, and therefore appropriate in this context.)

Listening to those Muslim pupils carefully articulate to me that they felt some staff were treating them differently because of their religion was hard to hear. As was the prayer room request – why hadn't I thought of it? I was supposed to be the Lead on Equality and Diversity and I hadn't thought of that. Self-judgement and guilt are natural, they will occur – but they are not the end result. That's just the sticky bit you have to go through to learn, grow and improve.

The power of apology here can go a long way: "Sorry, I got your pronoun wrong, I will remember next time."

Nearly every teacher I've ever met is a well-meaning person who wants the best for their pupils. To find out you were going about it the wrong way or made an assumption that was off the mark can be challenging for your ego. Also, just because a person may not have privilege in one way it doesn't mean they automatically understand the oppression of all minorities. Remember, it's only on television that we are 2D.

Some ways to finding your blindspots:

- Check who you are influenced by: if you only follow, watch, are friends with, and listen to people who have the same characteristics as you, how will you even know when you're in a bubble?
- Widen your circle of influence: and yes, this will take extra effort. Put into a search engine 'astronaut' for your lesson resources, and pictures of white, able bodied men come up. This is not representative of *all* astronauts. So in order to find anything different you will have to specify. This is the same with the films you watch on Netflix, the books you search for and the people you follow.

With this point we border on discussions of positive discrimination. Positive discrimination is the idea that we make favourable advantages for an underprivileged group on the theory that this will help to address the balance. So, think back to my friend who was in care who is unable to access university. Maybe a university notices this disadvantage and makes a fund that the young people leaving care can apply for. I am forbidden from applying to this fund. On paper, it looks wrong – they can get more free money than me – and maybe I don't have parents who can support financially anyway. These sorts of moral debates go around and around in many spheres – it is particularly acute when discussing land rights between races in America – how much of the country's past do you take into account? The land is a white man's, a Native American pays rent to live on it, however before the white man arrived it was a Native American's, however that was hundreds of years ago – it wasn't *that* white man who stole the land, and yet his current wealth (and privilege) stems from his ancestor's theft of that land … who should be paying rent to whom in the 21st century?

Back to widening your circle of influence – whichever side you fall on with the issue of positive discrimination (and that will be a moving point in itself), the fact remains that in order to be influenced by a group who is *not* the majority in your culture, you will have to dig a bit deeper. That does mean searching for 'Young adult fiction by Asian women', 'Films by female Directors' and 'Disabled, Brown Chefs' and so on.

Other ways to find blindspots:

- Survey, tally, audit – ask a pupil to simply tally who speaks during the lessons; who asks questions, who answers a question, who is chosen to speak – you can divide this by different characteristics.
- Check the diversity of your resources, references – on a themed day, for example International Women's Day, hide all the books on your shelves by men. What percentage of books are left? What does that show us? What messages does that send? Discuss with the pupils.
- Take a look at your behaviour points – who gets the most? Is there a pattern? Does a higher percentage go to your Pupil Premium Pupils, your EAL pupils or your SEND pupils? Why? What need is not being met? What's behind that behaviour?

- Who wins rewards? Look for patterns again. Do your pupils in care ever win rewards? What percentage of pupils of colour do you have in your class? Is the percentage who receive rewards in line with white pupils who receive rewards? Is there a correlation between who wins rewards and household income brackets? Why? What are you missing?
- Look at recruitment processes, staff representation; if certain groups aren't applying, why? What do you need to do? You may need to *actively* invite people in (positive discrimination). Also look at what type of roles different minorities do; for example, there are many Eastern European staff working in UK schools, very few of them are in Senior Leadership roles. Why? ("They just don't apply" is no longer good enough, what is the real or perceived barrier they face – ask, listen, believe, adapt.)
- Check the accessibility of outward facing communications. What percentage of your pupils are EAL? This can often suggest another language is spoken at home. Can those parents and carers access usual information?
- Provide *ongoing* training for staff from outside experts and people within the local community. Schools can get stuck in their own bubble. Step out, be prepared to learn from others.

INCLUSION AND SEND

The crossover between SEND needs and behavioural needs is complex and often misdiagnosed. The statistics show that a disproportionally high number of SEND pupils are excluded, which proves this. If we don't know our pupil's learning needs and account for them, they are more likely to disrupt. For a deeper study on this area, I recommend Jarlath O'Brien's (2016) poignant book *Don't Send Him in Tomorrow* in which he thoroughly investigates this area.

Interview

If you don't feel you belong, how safe can you be?

Pranav Patel usually goes by the name 'Pran' professionally – it is easier for most people to remember. 'Most' people in his professional world are white, British, English-only speakers. In one of his many poignant blogs he explains that as a pupil, one teacher went as far as asking if he could call him 'Peter' – to make it easier for the teacher.

In order to work in his home country's education system, Pranav must leave a little of himself at the school gates. Pranav Patel and I were born 47 miles away from each other in the Midlands. We have the same passport – British. Pranav is Brown. I am white.

(Continued)

For the purpose of this interview, I requested to call him by his actual name – I don't believe in making my school (book) gates a dumping ground for parts of people that don't match the majority.

Pranav has 17 years of teaching experience as a Physics teacher, an Assistant Principal and more recently, leads a movement to *Decolonise the Curriculum*. He supports leadership; leading standards; behaviour; data; professional development, and curriculum and is the forthcoming author of *The Anti Racist Teacher*.

Pranav has suffered from depression, anxiety and sleeplessness for much of his life; and understands first-hand the need for inclusive practices within education. Pranav stands as a mental health advocate; he recently featured in the BBC documentary 'Why teaching is making me ill' and has spoken openly about the pressure of the education sector.

Pranav begins with some definitions:

Inclusion: I think schools are families, and you don't *exclude* a family member, the aim is to include them in everything no matter what and accept them for whatever and everything that they are.

A definition of belonging that resonates strongly with Pranav is:

how much of you has to be left at the door when you enter a room. So as a pupil who's going through all these things, how much of them and whatever they're going through do they have to leave at the door? Do you allow them into that space? Do you allow a safe enough space for them to say "Sir/Miss, I feel … this is going on … I am … in my family … I speak …" and all of those things.

Next, the topic of unconscious bias:

Firstly, bias is bias, unconscious or not; damage is damage regardless of intention. The unconscious bit helps because it provides pillows, because it's hard to realise that "hold on, I've upheld kyriarchal structure for the last god-knows how long, and I benefit from that." So, people need pillows to be put into that place. But we need to have the recognition that we must be really careful with that word "oh, it was unconscious, there's nothing I can do about it." It's a dangerous and unhelpful thought.

Pranav shares the academic term for bias:

It is not necessarily a bad thing, it's a habit to the mind; it's to save cognitive energy. The problem is when it impacts others' lives or our organisation. The unconscious part of this is when you're brought up into a world that denigrates certain groups and normalises others.

Exemplifying this, Pranav refers to films, "when do I ever see an Asian guy or a Black person as a ballet dancer? When do I ever see a Black character as the brains behind an organisation?" demonstrating that our western normalisation is not neutral.

Bias interplays on every single relationship we have. It is the same with every characteristic. If you were talking to me and I was a trans female or someone who identified as non-binary, this conversation would be completely different because the environment completely changes depending on your experiences with said group.

Moving this into the classroom, we can see how bias (unconscious or not) will inevitably affect how we interact with different pupils with different characteristics in our class – depending on our past experience of being with people of that characteristic – positive or negative. When we give out those behaviour or reward points, we are not neutral. Bias is always interplaying in our relationships. Pranav goes on to explain that this is not necessarily a problem if we are *aware* of it:

you are better off thinking, "I have this bias, I am now going to mitigate it." So in recruitment when I hire people, I have a fierce conversation with myself, I use Susan Scott's method with myself, "you know you are biased towards […] what was actually said in the interview?"

How do we find our blindspots? Pranav gives an insightful answer:

Look at your data, your behaviour sanctions and your feelings around behaviour and groups. I advocate a 'words not tone' policy. So as a Senior Leader, I don't want to read the story and opinion, I want to know what words were said in each incident. The process of typing out what was said, in the schools that I work, causes the defiance figures to drop off, because what you're doing is moving from the original bias and moving towards a rational process to find out what was actually said.

As a Brown educator advocating for an anti-racist education system, Pranav must be armed with facts and statistics to prove the points he knows experientially to be true, otherwise people don't believe him:

Black boys with SEND are 168 times more likely to be excluded. In the year 2018, 56% of Gypsy, Roma, Traveller were excluded; over half of an ethnic group. Black boys from Caribbean Heritage are 2.2 times more likely to be assessed with an SEMH than a white pupil.

I asked Pranav how these statistics have become true, speaking from the pupil's perspective:

Your teachers' ability to judge you academically directly links to your behaviour. So, if I mess around more my teacher thinks I'm worse academically than where I am. So then guess what happens, I'm bored in class, or my teacher doesn't think a lot of me, I mess around a bit more, my teacher's ability gets worse again, they think I'm below, and then you're caught on a spiral all the way down. I don't think there's any malice on that,

(Continued)

but we're caught up in this loop. If we're all anchored around black men and boys being aggressive in gangs, guess what we see? The way needs (and exclusions) are assessed in schools is by observation; observation prompted by bias.

In attempting to readdress the bias, interestingly Pranav does not go by the old adage: 'Start afresh in every classroom', instead:

I don't advocate that because it's impossible. You're better off saying, "this kid annoys the hell out of me, so when I do have an interaction, I'm going to have that in the back of mind." You don't forget about it, you hold it, so you think, "is this that person being intentionally cantankerous or is it me?"

Finally, how do we get past being tokenistic?

I advocate changing your culture. Let everyone bring everything to the table, bring in everything that they are and will be and can be into the room. Instead of saying this is our culture and we will hammer you into this culture of compliance, or we will get rid of you, you need to incorporate the culture into a joint melting pot – because that is what true belonging is.

And how does the teacher create that melting pot, where do we start?

Listen. Sit and listen and talk to the children.

Ultimately behaviour for me is a game of people, and if you don't have safety – which is essentially belonging – and inclusion, you don't really have an environment that fosters relationships. Learning is a relational practice. Almost all learning is a social act.

Source: Interview with author, 2020

Action Box

Next lesson

Go through your social media feed. Look at the percentage of people you follow (and are therefore influenced by every time you pick up your phone) who do *not* have your characteristics. Add ten new people who are different to you.

Next week

Use the 'Power Flower' tool to learn about social divisions as a way to understand your own privilege and oppression and recognise how this will inform how you teach. Also suitable as a teaching resource for pupils in secondary schools. For more info and to download follow this link: http://lgbtq2stoolkit.learningcommunity.ca/wp/wp-content/uploads/2014/12/flower-power-exercise.pdf (accessed March 26, 2021).

Long term

Create a system with your behaviour and reward points that allows you to monitor by characteristics of the pupils. Review it regularly and ask the questions: *Why? What are we missing? What are the unmet needs? What can we do to address this?* If possible, make this school-wide.

What has any of this got to do with behaviour?

I hope that this link has become clear. But just in case you need a succinct quote for an essay:

If a pupil does not feel safe, included or as if they belong, they will experience extra barriers to learning. Often these barriers show themselves as behaviour that challenges the adults around them.

Further reading

Defying Disaffection: How Schools Are Winning The Hearts and Minds of Reluctant Students – Reva Klein (2000)

Pulling from examples across the UK and the US, Klein examines the barriers to inclusion that young people with behavioural needs face, and proven ways schools are positively tackling this. This book was also one of the catalysts for me to write this one.

(Continued)

Infantilising Disabled People Is a Thing and You're Probably Unconsciously Doing It – Elizabeth Wright (2020)

Elizabeth has a whole host of fascinating and useful articles for both able and disabled bodied people to read. As an able-bodied person, I find she addresses the questions I'm too scared to ask – gold dust for educators. Most articles are available on Medium or one of the online magazines she edits, *Disability Review Magazine* and *Conscious Being*.

Don't Send Him in Tomorrow – Jarlath O'Brien (2016)

A heart-wrenching and important book that offers an improved approach to school structures that ensures pupils with SEND have an equal chance at education in the UK.

The Antiracist Educator – Pran Patel (2022)

Forthcoming with Sage, a practical guide on how educators can do better in schools, backed up by theory, research and evidence.

Big Gay Adventures in Education – contributor Adele Bates, Editor Daniel Tomlinson-Gray (2021)

A collation of experiences from LGBTQ+ teachers and pupils highlighting how being LGBTQ+ still very much affects the way you can teach and learn in British schools.

8

"MISS, DO YOU LIVE IN THIS CLASSROOM?": BE PART OF A TEAM

#INSULTOFTHEWEEK

Me: "How was your half term?"
Pupil: "Like you."
Me: "Like me? What do you mean?"
Pupil: "Boring."

IN THIS CHAPTER YOU WILL

- Discover the many aspects, areas and people who can be called upon as your supportive team.
- Find where you have holes in your support.

INTRODUCTION

Teaching can be lonely. Whilst you may be surrounded by the equivalent of a small village, on days where behaviour is getting you down and you look out onto a sea of small (or not so small) faces, expecting *you* to know what to do, it can feel very isolating. The double-edged experience of feeling completely responsible and yet completely helpless are familiar. If you are lucky, you're based in a school where a quick trip to the department office or staffroom can provide a whole host of support from colleagues who, just by the gait of your walk, can tell you need some love and tea. Unfortunately though, many of us don't make it to the staffroom – you've got a lunchtime detention, you've got marking piled high and you have no idea what you're doing with 8FR last thing. Worst of all, some schools suffer from an excess of hostility and competition. No one notices that you haven't left your classroom in three weeks, because everyone else is doing the same and the atmosphere amongst staff is one of competition rather than camaraderie. Teachers in these kinds of unfavourable conditions rarely last long and I know that unfortunately some believe that *they* are the main problem, that teaching isn't for them and so they are added to the pile of 1/3 of teachers who plan to leave the profession (TES, 2021).

If this is you, hold on.

There are also stories of people hitting this rock bottom, throwing out a lifeline to work in a different school and discovering a practically whole new job where they feel safe, supported, inspired and able to be the kind of teacher they intended to be.

A fantastic colleague of mine had spent nearly twenty years in one mainstream school, building her way up to SLT. When it got taken over for academisation there were huge clashes in her vision for education and the new way she was being directed to teach. She despaired and felt she had lost her place. She was unsure how she would fit in, and whether she wanted to go through similar experiences elsewhere. Then she saw a job advertised for a special SEMH school. She gave it a go. She felt she had landed her dream job – to be back in an environment that put relationships first, working with some of the most challenging behaviour from pupils across the city – I have not to this day seen her without a beaming smile across her face whilst at work (and that includes during COVID-19 measures).

The bottom line here, whatever situation you are in, is that we all need support and to feel part of something bigger. Behaviour challenging you in the classroom is one thing, but if you know that follow ups will happen, management or Heads support you, there is a robust behaviour or relationship policy consistently used throughout the school, and communication with parents and carers is easily set up, then it can become manageable – possibly even enjoyable. Ensure you have a team at all levels, look for your gaps and find ways to fill them.

TEAM AROUND THE CHILD (TAC)

For most mainstream pupils this team is almost invisible. They will have their teachers, Head of Year or pastoral and hopefully a fairly supportive adult or two at home. Other pupils, however, will need much more support for their learning, medical or mental health needs, trauma, neglect or abuse they have experienced or are still experiencing.

When the pupils do not have the additional team they need, they will not be able to function as well in your lessons, which may well lead to behaviour issues. Below is a list of adult roles (and there may be more) who could be involved in supporting your pupils. Link with them, communicate concerns and successes – this will provide you with vast amounts of information, ideas and support for when things get tough:

- Key worker in school
- Teaching Assistant
- Pupil Premium Lead
- SENCO
- Educational Psychologist
- Occupational Therapist
- Doctors
- First language/translator support
- Intervention teachers
- Social Worker
- Therapist
- Counsellor
- Youth Worker
- Drugs/alcohol/substance abuse support worker
- Mentors or Buddies in or outside of school
- Foster carers or respite foster carers
- Parents and extended family
- Children's home link worker
- CAHMS
- Mental health support worker
- Virtual School (for Looked After Children)
- Family support worker

Alternatively, if you feel a pupil may need additional support and it's not in place, you can ask for it. Due to lack of resources, funding and time it may be that you have to ask several times – don't be afraid to be a nuisance. Unfortunately, it is the pupils who have someone advocating on behalf of them who are most likely to get the support they need, not the ones in the most need. We joke that as teachers we play all these roles ourselves, and sometimes it's necessary, but in the long term, if a pupil requires support outside of your teaching remit, it is best for them to have professionals in each field – that way you can concentrate on what you do best: teaching.

A NOTE ON JOB TITLES

Job titles of course can be useful, however, in my experience they only reveal a tiny bit of what the person is or isn't capable of. I have worked with a leader with one year's experience who couldn't give me any support with behaviour, an SLT who undermined my behaviour approaches with a pupil (which resulted in an extra three weeks of rebuilding the relationship), and I have also had the pleasure of working with many Teaching Assistants who can 'do behaviour' with their little finger – whilst simultaneously driving the minibus, making the lunches, knowing every pupil *and* their parent or carer and running the Christmas Fayre with a special *Frozen* theme this year with a tombola sponsored by 37 local businesses.

The best way to work out where support might be is by asking and trusting. Whilst the pupil's TA may not have the qualifications, they may have worked with that pupil one-to-one for four years, which will be a vital source of knowledge for you.

Once I was working in an SEMH school, I was put in a situation that ideally should not have happened. But it did, there were various breakdowns in communication from the school's part, and I share this experience as I know this will be happening elsewhere too.

I walked into a classroom to meet a new pupil. I entered with my usual bouncy welcome. His face was like thunder. First he threw his pen at me. Whilst attempting to remain pleasant, I lay the boundary that this wasn't acceptable and let's start again. He proceeded to throw his chair at me. This was the first time the pupil had met me, so I knew (at least) that this wasn't personal. As I tried again to engage in reasonable conversation, the TA working with him turned to me sternly and asked me to leave. On paper this shouldn't happen – a TA telling a teacher what to do, a teacher leaving the pupil when she should be teaching them, a TA being left in a room alone with a volatile pupil. *But* it was exactly the right thing to do. I walked away feeling a little shaken and confused, both by the violence of the pupil and the sternness of the TA. However, I also knew that this TA was extremely experienced at working with pupils with SEMH pupils, she had also been working at this school for years, whereas I had been there just less than a year. In that moment I took the decision to trust her judgement rather than mine. To trust my instinct that told me that she would only direct me so firmly if it were important. It turned out to be spot on. As soon as she could, the TA came to find me and explained the situation. This pupil had been very badly sexually and physically abused at home. We were his umpteenth attempt at education, and he had a deep distrust of adults. New adults were not safe. So, as I had suspected, there was nothing personal about this interchange.

New Adult = potential threat

Action = get them away as soon as possible

It's a sensible strategy if that is what your family history has taught you before the age of ten years – just to remain alive.

The TA then also explained to me that my jovial attempt to re-instate boundaries was triggering the pupil. She had already seen the signs of it a few times before that week with other staff, and she could see it building again. She told me to leave to keep both me and the pupil safe. Once he was calm with her again, they discussed his actions towards me and explained why they weren't good. I thanked her.

Yes, my ego felt bruised: "but I hadn't done anything to the pupil, how could she know better than me when I was supposed to be the teacher? Isn't it important to hold boundaries? Are we going to allow pupils to hurt staff? Wasn't I supposed to be 'good' at behaviour?" – that was irrelevant mind chatter. Sometimes we are stripped to the basic important thing; keeping our young people and ourselves safe. In order to do this we might sometimes need to step back and pass the baton on. The prevention for this scene would have been a more robust communication process about new pupils across the school (insuring part time staff were included, which I was at the time), and pre-planning around how, who and when the pupil would meet new staff.

TEAM AROUND YOU

COLLEAGUES

There are different types of support you will need from your colleagues. Some will be professional, the mentors or line managers who (hopefully) support and enable you to do your job in a practical and logistical way. But you need more than this. You need colleagues who are also able to support you emotionally. Teaching can be a tough job. Add onto that some personal difficulties or a global pandemic, and it becomes a seemingly impossible job. Everyone reacts differently to pressure and support will look different for each of us, but we still need it. Do you have colleagues who you can go to for:

- Professional advice
- Fun
- Emotional support
- Practical support
- Tech support
- Distraction?

What to do if not?

You need to find this support elsewhere. Online is of course a great source for this and #EduTwitter used in the right way can be a community of colleagues (just know where your boundaries are and only do it if it feels good – watch out for getting sucked in). During the lockdown of 2020 I became part of a group that formed, the Education Wellbeing Collective, who came together to support one another through the very unusual time, and to support and champion the evolution of wellbeing in schools and their communities. One result of the group has been *The Big Book of Whole School Wellbeing* (Evans et al., 2022), another has been engagement with politicians about the best approaches to 'catching up' for our pupils after lockdowns. Whilst we came together as professionals, we found great emotional support with one another as we got used to working isolated in lockdown, and to supporting schools, pupils, carers and parents in a way that had never previously been asked of us. There were some weeks that our meetings felt like a lifeline for me.

There are other sources of support that you can seek, which are outlined below:

- **Education Support** – A charity in the UK that provides mental health and wellbeing support to staff in education. They have BACP qualified counsellors available 24 hours. educationsupport.org.uk
- **Teacher Support** – Empowering teachers with options. Presenting you with CPD, career opportunities (or alternatives), ways to diversify your income and more. www.teacherempowermentproject.co.uk/
- **WomenEd** – Connecting aspiring/existing women leaders in global education. @WomenEd
- **BAME Ed** – Working to ensure visible diversity in education. Open to *all* people. Join us to network, to gain support and advice. BAMEednetwork.com

- **LGBT Ed** – Empowering LGBT+ educators to be visible and authentic in schools for the benefit of LGBT+ young people. lgbted.uk
- **Disability Ed** – Group to include everyone as educators. https://disabilityeduk.org
- Teaching Unions:

  o   For Teaching Assistants and support staff: UNISON www.unison.org.uk
  o   For teachers: NEU neu.org.uk and NASUWT www.nasuwt.org.uk
  o   For headteachers: NAHT www.naht.org.uk

- For educators in Local Authorities, academies or private workplaces: Voice Community www.voicetheunion.org.uk/who-we-support (all websites accessed March28, 2021).

Outside of school you also need a team. Some of those people will be someone you can talk to about school, others will be those types of wonderful or infuriating friends who never ask you anything about your work. Do you have:

- Emotional support
- Fun people
- Spiritual and wellbeing support
- Family or chosen family support
- Support for particular physical or mental health issues
- Additional support for particularly challenging times?

A NOTE TO SUPPLY TEACHERS

Firstly, you are amazing, thank you.

In my time as a supply teacher, I have been ignored, sniggered at, undermined and looked down upon – *all in the staffroom by other staff.* Supply teachers are often welcomed with suspicion. Sometimes they are the only people even sat in the staffroom able to have lunch – which can be acutely felt as jealous eyes look over at your full 21 minutes to eat and 4pm leaving time. And I'm sure I'm guilty of this myself as a permanent teacher – investing in another welcome and positive relationship can be an ask too much when stress is high and that supply teacher will be replaced by another person the following day.

Supply teachers, this is why you need to look after yourself even more and find your team. You are often in fire-fighting situations in the classroom, left with the boring lesson plans that no one wants to do. It's not an easy task.

When approaching a new school *do* get the 1, 2, 3 on how the behaviour or relationship policy works in the school, and who to contact if everything goes wobbly. There is no shame in this. You have very little time to establish a relationship with a class, and so you are more likely to face challenging behaviour (as Allan Ahlberg's (1984) poem *The Supply Teacher* so beautifully and excruciatingly illustrates).

Without a consistent community or friendship group within a school it is important you strengthen these connections outside of school. Contact some of the groups listed above (you can still be a part of a teachers' union) if you don't know where to start with this. Supply teaching can have a *lot* of advantages (lunch; a finishing time), but you still need support to make it sustainable.

TEAM APPROACHES TO BEHAVIOUR

There are a few approaches now used in schools that make use of colleagues working together in order to support behaviour. Team Teach is a widely recognised training provider that develops and promotes positive behaviour management strategies which:

> emphasise team building, personal safety, communication, and verbal and non-verbal de-escalation techniques for dealing with challenging behaviour which reduce the need for physical intervention. (Team Teach, 2021)

They also teach positive handling techniques as a last resort. It is worth looking into this or similar behaviour trainings as a whole staff if behaviour is a schoolwide issue (see more in Chapter 9).

RESTORATIVE PRACTICE

Restorative Justice and Practice is now widely used in schools alongside behaviour approaches. It is a way of allowing pupils to become accountable and responsible for their behaviour, rather than solely being punished (and often repeating the behaviour). The Restorative Justice Council is the main voice across the UK. They describe how:

> [...] Restorative Justice is used by Headteachers proactively to build relationships, promote discipline and prevent harm and conflict occurring. Restorative Justice builds on existing practice, including the use of circles, mediation skills and peer mediation training for the children. It goes on to develop both informal and formal procedures such as one-to-one support in order to decide the best approach to meet the needs of the school and pupils. It is also used as a response by schools to enforce discipline whilst emphasising the value of positive relationships and active citizenship. (Restorative Justice Council, 2011: 1)

'Restorative Justice' and 'Restorative Practice' are often used interchangeably, however Tyler Brewster and Shana Louallen give us a useful differentiation:

> Restorative Justice (RJ) is a community-based approach to building, repairing and restoring relationships. At its best, RJ provides a space for community members to be held accountable while participating in creating pathways to repair.

[...] Restorative practices, often used interchangeably with RJ, refer to specific responses within a community that aim to build capacity for members to discuss, dissect and challenge individual perspectives. (Brewster and Louallen, 2016)

Ofsted are supportive of RJ practices in school. It is evident also that schools who are also able to link to the wider team of local authorities and outside agencies have a stronger impact with the practice. Notably, RJ has been found to considerably lower the rates of exclusions in schools and increase staff confidence in working together to support and manage behaviour (Restorative Justice Council, 2011). The Department of Education published a report on *The Use and Effectiveness of Anti-bullying Strategies in Schools* that found that Restorative Practices had the highest rates of effectiveness for dealing with bullying (Thompson and Smith, 2010).

The emphasis on how to implement a Restorative approach in schools lies with well trained staff. I thoroughly recommend asking for this training and learning more. This figure below illustrates clearly how supportive this approach can be in preventing and dealing with challenging behaviour.

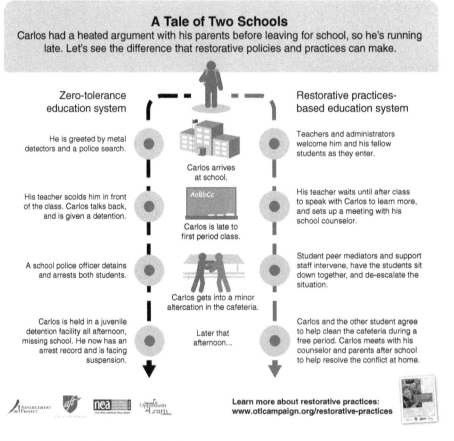

Figure 8.1   A tale of two schools

Source: The Schott Foundation for Public Education

Throughout the entire day it is clear how the team around the child, working together with an understanding approach, are able to support Carlos' behaviour. Notably on the Restorative side, Carlos is welcomed by not just teachers but also administrators. PRUs and APs often do this as common practice, which makes such a difference to the pupils' day and their ability to learn. A school's leaders will have consciously thought about the kind of community they want to foster; the administrators are not shoved in an office somewhere, detached from the young people they are working for, but instead are known by pupils – so the pupils can learn that they are surrounded by safe adults. In addition, the teachers and administrators work as a team, not just around the admin, but in the school's overall ethos of supporting the young people. On the Restorative side Carlos' teacher calls upon the school counsellor – another professional, to help get to the bottom of Carlos' lateness. The teacher knows when to pass on, and the school's infrastructure enables this.

In Restorative Practice the pupils themselves are involved in restoration, which gives them understanding and experience of resolving conflict – key skills they will need as adults.

At the end of the day on the Restorative side, the team connections extend further, to home and professionals, which not only enables Carlos to understand that he has supportive adults around him who work together and care, but also provides the web of connection for the adults themselves.

THE FINNISH MODEL OF TEAM IN EDUCATION

During my education research trip to Finland, one of the most stark contrasts between the UK and Finnish education that I found was the infrastructure of professionals in and around the schools. *By law* in Finland they are required to have:

* One SEND Qualified to Masters Level Teacher for every 200 students – so five to six on-site full time in an average city secondary school of around 1000 pupils.

Per 800 pupils:

* One full-time Counsellor
* One part-time Psychotherapist
* One part-time Social Worker
* One part-time Nurse (all teachers have First Aid training)

It is against the law to set the students by ability in schools.

The result is astounding, and also busts a myth about Finnish education: many people think that the Finns are a progressive lot, and that classrooms are radically different to the UK. Yes, some are. But in the month I spent there, visiting several schools, I saw the same variety of teaching quality and styles as the UK (some car crash lessons, some incredible lessons). The difference was the team around the teacher, that *enabled the teacher to teach.* When a pupil shows signs of not being able to work, whatever the reason, the teacher calls on one of the on-site professionals to help.

The pupil will have regular time booked in with them, the professional can spend time getting to the bottom of the issue *outside* of the formal learning in the classroom. If the professional feels it would help the pupil's overall progress in education, they will return to the teacher discussing a programme of work for a set period of time in which the pupil does not need to cover the curriculum. In many of the interviews I had with health professionals, social workers, counsellors, psychologists and teachers, they all had the same approach – it was better to not quite cover six weeks' worth of curriculum in order to reset the pupil onto a positive path to learning for the rest of their education.

In addition, their approach to SEND is radically different to ours. Of all pupils in Finnish schools, 25% receive SEND support during their school path – because they help first and only diagnose if needed. So a child can receive immediate bespoke intervention on site, often saving years of struggle before they can get the Dyslexia/ADHD/Autism/Dyspraxia/Speech and Language delay diagnosis that we wait for in the UK.

It is also worth noting that in Finland private schools and private tutoring are illegal. Their approach is to have an inclusive education *for all* – and put in the resources, professionals and infrastructure to support it.

Finally, a Finnish school's team extends past the school gates. Schools meet regularly within their network (usually equivalent to the Local Authority); and vitally, all of the non-teaching professionals are directly linked to the city or district's services. So, for example, if the school Social Worker believes there are issues at home for a child that needs further investigation, it's one call to their colleagues in the local social services or they bring it up on the day a week they spend in that office. The same with the psychologist and nurse.

All of this careful planning in infrastructure (re-developed in the 1970s in Finland, part of a huge national decision of self-development post-Russian involvement in Finland), enables teachers to teach – and guess what?

The pupils learn.

For teachers and schools in the UK this can be an enviable set up as already stretched resources struggle to give pupils the wraparound support they need. However, it is possible – read the interviews in Chapter 9 for more.

BE A TEAM PLAYER FOR OTHERS

Finally, whilst you may not be or plan to be in Finland, there are still things you can do in your own setting. One of them is to be there for others – this is a two-way thing. Some reminders:

- Trainees and NQTs: they are often terrified; of the pupils, their lessons *and* what you think of them. How can you help?
- Supply teachers: remember walking into the school for the first time and getting lost and not knowing anyone? How can you help?
- Managers and SLT: they may have a title; they may fit it, they may not. They have extra responsibilities. They can also have bad days and personal challenges. How can you help?

- Headteachers: they are at the top, and therefore alone. Many Heads feel lonely in the big decisions they must make on behalf of the school community, and feel that they can't been seen to be asking for help from their staff. How can you help?
- Support staff: they may be inexperienced or much more experienced than you. How are they being treated in your classrooms? You could learn from them, they may need your guidance. How can you help?
- Admin and other staff around the school: many of these staff don't have quite the same love of education and pupils that most teaching staff do. They may not understand children, they may be intimidated when you leave one in their office for two minutes whilst you nip to the photocopier. Or maybe they'd love to work with pupils more but are unsure how to approach them. How can you help?

I am not advocating that you spend all your time helping all staff, but sometimes that five-minute chat can mean so much. In addition, as Frederika mentioned in Chapter 1, linking with others gives us meaning, which is one of the ways we can ensure our own wellbeing is topped up.

Interview

> It's all about balance [...] It's about being very clear at the start of the year that everyone struggles at some point, what you are doing is tough [...] it is rewarding, but it is a hungry job that is never done, it's a noisy job.

Dr Emma Kell has over 20 years' experience as a teacher and leader at middle and senior level. Dr Emma works as Senior Teaching Fellow at UCL's Institute of Education and as an English teacher and Teaching School Lead role for Aspire AP, a PRU in Bucks.

I was introduced to Dr Emma as a fellow TEDx speaker, who regularly speaks and writes on wellbeing, recruitment and retention. With such a variety of experience in different roles within schools, I was keen to speak with Dr Emma specifically about her experience of teams in schools from different angles.

She began with her experience with behaviour as a TA:

> I was absolutely clueless, I had zero training, zero skills in anything, I used to be able to put up backing paper. But I have a distinct memory of working with small groups, going to the teacher and saying "Christopher's being naughty again". The teacher would ask "but what is he doing?" I didn't have the language to be able to say "he's interrupting me again or he's struggling with the learning." All I could see was a child not doing what he was told.

(Continued)

I wonder how many untrained staff feel the same in our schools still now? Interestingly, in her first teaching post, Dr Emma described being "terrified" of two particular girls and "feeling quite lonely." I asked if she'd felt as if she'd been offered any support at this early stage of her career. Her response is a common one:

I didn't ask for help. I didn't know that everybody struggled. I didn't know to ask for help, so I didn't.

Later Dr Emma moved to what was at the time the "lowest achieving school in the area, which had the highest number of refugees in a school in Europe." She described it as:

Rough as boots – and I absolutely loved it. I got told to f*** off once a week at least, regular fights – but the staff were amazing. There was a real sense of solidarity and teamwork. I think that's when I came to love my job.

Unfortunately, Dr Emma's experience as SLT for five years wasn't always quite so rosy. Of note here, it was not to do with the pupils or the behaviour, but the unwritten rules that went with the role and who she was supposed to be within the school team.

I like to be able to have a laugh with staff and get to know people really well and show my own vulnerabilities. But the time and place when I was SLT, those things were quite frowned upon. There were some extremely prescriptive measures that came in for behaviour, and we had to go around and check and we had to report staff and they would get told off. So for me it was enacting stuff I didn't believe. I'm not sure as a member of SLT I would have been allowed to be seen to ask for help.

I asked what her worst and best examples of teams in a school were that she had witnessed throughout her career. The worst example was:

Behaviour points being used as a stick to beat teachers with, particularly new teachers. Teachers being put on 'a cause for concern' as a result of dishing out too many behaviour points to students. The result of that was varied: one member of staff ended up leaving, what other staff did was stop giving the behaviour points and close their doors and stop asking for help because they knew they were going to be shamed and made to feel incompetent. There was no staffroom, so you'd have people simply not knowing each other from one part of the school to the other.

And the best example was:

A school with significant challenges, but right from the outset there was a real sense of "we trust you as a teacher and we've got your back. Regardless of your rank you're going to struggle at some point with student behaviour and we are here for you." They had an on-call system where there were constantly people around the corridors at all times and those people were an incredibly diverse staff, so there was a sense of representing the same level of diversity as the students, so there were staff of all different colours, all different ages. You always had this safety net because there was an acknowledgement that our students were challenging. That sense that you're not on your own. People around all the time popping their heads in and out all the time, just saying hi and coming in to join in with a couple moments of the lesson.

It's a bit like a relationship between the staff member and the school; if the ethos doesn't suit you and the values aren't shared then it goes very toxic very quickly and it can make you ill and it can be incredibly damaging for the mental health of the individual concerned, but also to their immediate team members.

Dr Emma often discusses the moral compass of a school team. She feels that you need to share this, but:

that doesn't necessarily mean approaching aims in the same way. So as a team, you don't want people who are going to think you're brilliant all the time or who say yes to you all the time or see the world in the same way. Teachers often clash with one another, when it comes to jobs with a very strong sense of moral purpose.

Dr Emma is a big Tweeter, so I asked her how much she thought Twitter could be a source of support and team for those teachers who don't have the support in school. Her response was immediate: "Oh my god, it has literally changed my life." She started on Twitter as part of her research for her doctorate on teacher wellbeing and work-life balance.

The level of engagement meant I was starting to have conversations with people about the struggles of being a parent and being a teacher. I came across people who then, when I had my year from hell, were so there for me, not on the public Twitter forum but behind the scenes of Twitter, that my ability to then privately message those people and say "actually I'm really struggling" and for those people to scoop me up.

If it wasn't for those Twitter networks, I wouldn't have left the school that was making me so miserable.

Finally, Dr Emma emphasised the importance of staff having "structured space to listen and be heard." If you don't feel you have this in your role, please reach out.

Source: Interview with author, 2020

Action Box

Next lesson

Have a look at the list for 'Team around you'. Do you feel you have a good mixture of support? Where are the gaps? Reach out, put them in place now (even if you don't feel you need them right now, they'll be ready when you do).

Next week

Think of one to two pupils whose behaviour is challenging for you. Consider the needs they have. What support could be put in place for them to be able to function in your classes more successfully? Investigate what team they have around them, are there gaps? Are there professionals in their life who could help you understand the pupil's behaviour in your class? Reach out.

Long term

Seek additional behaviour training either for yourself, a small team or schoolwide. Spend some time researching further about Restorative Practices and envisioning how they could fit in your community.

What has any of this got to do with behaviour?

As Dr Emma Kell's career so clearly demonstrates; having the right team around you can help you deal with the most challenging behaviour, and still enjoy the job. I've experienced it too; it is definitely possible.

Further reading

How to Survive in Teaching: Without Imploding, Exploding or Walking Away – Dr Emma Kell (2018)

One of Dr Emma's books that offers practical advice, support and positive approaches to entering and staying in the profession.

Restorative Justice Council

The British organisation supporting Restorative Justice, they specifically provide support for schools. https://restorativejustice.org.uk (accessed March 26, 2021).

What on Earth Makes Finnish Schools so Good? – Adele Bates

https://adelebateseducation.co.uk/what-on-earth-makes-finnish-schools-so-good/ (accessed March 26, 2021).

Finnish Education: Part 2 – Adele Bates

https://adelebateseducation.co.uk/finnish-education-part-2/ (accessed March 26, 2021).

Finnish Education: Balance for Better – Part 3 – Adele Bates

https://adelebateseducation.co.uk/finnish-education-balance-for-better-part-3/ (accessed March 26, 2021).

A three-part series of blog posts and vlogs about the Finnish Education system, including the schoolwide infrastructure, roles and wages.

9

"MISS, THIS SCHOOL IS DEAD": SCHOOLWIDE APPROACHES TO BEHAVIOUR

#INSULTOFTHEWEEK

Discussing a member of staff who is leaving at the end of term –

Me: "How do you feel about that?"
Pupil: "Annoyed."
Me: "Oh dear, why's that?"
Pupil: "Because it's not you."

IN THIS CHAPTER YOU WILL

- Consider behaviour from a schoolwide, leadership perspective.
- Understand the first steps you need to take to sustain or change the culture of behaviour across a whole school.
- Learn specific approaches and strategies that you may want to adopt schoolwide.

INTRODUCTION

First of all, find out what's actually going on from the children's perspective.

Not only what your behaviour policy says, not only what the governors say, not even what the teachers say at this point. Find out what school is like for those pupils who are 'known' for their behaviour. There is a very simple way to do this – spend a day in their shoes.

A DAY IN THEIR SHOES

Choose a pupil to follow and observe them for a day. It's best not to tell them directly (that will freak them out), but let the class know that you'll be around that day. Also, let the teaching staff know what you're doing, and that your focus is on the pupils. The logistics are easy, here's the hard bit:

We all know that the observer in a room changes everything, and as a known leader in the school you most likely will affect both how pupils and staff are in a classroom. Some of that can't be helped, but what you can do is – and this will be challenging – switch off your job role and *actually* observe. Your only objective is to understand how this pupil experiences your school – no grading, no objectives, no feedback, no intervention *unless* requested.

Be the fly on the wall – *I dare you.*

Also, a warning, the first time I did this I cannot believe how tiring it was. Just observing a six period day? Sounds super easy but the amount of revelations and realisations I had per second was incredible. Take a notepad and pen.

Other tips to get the most out of this:

• Put an out of office on your emails.
• Do *not* check your emails.
• Let anyone who is likely to call you know that you are 'out' for the day.

If a lesson is boring, or you see the pupil become disengaged, it is important that you experience this too. They (most likely) will not be allowed their phone for distraction; we cannot tell pupils that they should concentrate in a situation we can't ourselves. Also, what does it tell us about the level of engagement or differentiation in our teaching if *we* feel the need to distract? Often a pupil has felt this need before an adult and – oopsy daisy, if there is no outlet, you get some distracting behaviour. Leave the ipad/phone/doodee watch in your office – dare to really see what's going on, the huffs, the learning needs not met, the exact second where you see the disengagement happen – why? Did they have lunch? Is this the third teacher in three lessons who has not said a positive thing to the pupil? How would that make you feel? How does a six period day on someone else's time and expectations feel? Look for the nuances.

Other ways to find out what's really going on are listed below. Before embarking on any of them decide what you want to know – is it a general understanding of behaviour from different perspectives? It is specific opinions about a new part of a behaviour policy? Experience of a specific location, time or lesson in school? Be conscious of asking loaded questions, more conscientious staff and pupils may already be telling you what they think you want to hear. Ensure that there is also space for 'any other comments' – sometimes the tidbits that participants give as an afterthought are the most revealing.

STUDENT CONSULTATION

As mentioned in Chapter 7, in my longer behaviour programmes, I always add this section, and it is always the most insightful activity for teaching staff. You may start this discussion with the school council or student voice group, but be mindful of the range of 'types' of pupils you are including in your consultation. Often it is not the pupils with behaviour that challenges adults who volunteer or have the opportunity for such student representation roles.

How will you get to the pupils who are often not in school? How will you ensure that the demographic of your answers matches the demographic of your school? i.e. what percentage of pupils in care/EAL/SEND/pupils of colour or other ethnicity do you have in your school? What percentage of them have participated in your consultations? You will need to adapt – some pupils will need one-to-one discussions, some an online survey, some will need help understanding the questions, some will only participate with staff they know – be creative. *Differentiate.* This process will give you different information to the observation day.

Table 9.1 shows some suggested questions to get you started.

Table 9.1   Suggested questions to get you started

• For pupils, what should/ could the school be? – And why?	• An educational space • A community space • A social space • Other – please explain
• We're going to list some things; please tell us if they should be allowed in school in your opinion, and why:	• Loud swearing • Drugs • Alcohol • Hot food in lessons • Shouting • Rearranging furniture • Running • Lateness to lessons • Backchatting • Talking to friends in lessons • Prejudice language, e.g. homophobic, racist, ableist etc.

• What other guidelines do you have on how pupils should behave:	• In lessons? • In the yard? • Outside of school with school uniform on? • Towards staff? • Towards each other? • Towards pupils who are breaking rules?
• What do you think the three most important rules should be around behaviour in schools?	
• What do you think should be the consequences for not sticking to those rules?	
• What, in your opinion, are effective incentives for behaviour?	
• What guidelines do you have on how staff should behave:	• Towards pupils in general? • Towards pupils exceeding expectations? • Towards each other?
• How much should parents and carers be involved in their child's behaviour?	
• We're going to describe a situation in school. Please explain:	1. What you think about it. 2. What should be done by the staff in the moment. 3. Anything that needs to change in school to prevent these things happening? (Then use some real case studies that have happened recently, maybe ones the pupils will be aware of.)

Also re-read the questions I asked pupils for the Foreword of this book for more ideas.

STAFF CONSULTATION

Importantly, ensure this is a *staff* consultation and not a *teacher* consultation. Notoriously, behaviour can often be the most challenging for the staff the least trained to deal with it – the lunchtime supervisors, cleaners, admin staff – they are also staff who observe a lot and may give you different perspectives of the reality.

Again, be sensitive as to how you set this up. Don't rely on only a face-to-face meeting, there will be people in the room who will not feel confident to answer or critique. Blend the responses with an anonymous survey. In addition, you could have an agreed set of three to five questions that you ask everyone who enters your office for a week, maybe one or two that you ask of every member of staff you spend more than a minute with. Use a many-pronged approach. One thirty-minute discussion with staff in the staffroom (which is only ever the same select staff usually) will not give you a real picture. Importantly, seek out those members of staff you don't see – why does the NQT or the teacher who is about to retire hide in their room?

Some suggestions:

- Do you feel this school has a positive culture of behaviour? Why/why not?
- Which areas do you feel are the best (time, place or activity)?
- Which areas do you feel are the worst (time, place or activity)?
- Do you feel adequately trained to deal with the types of behaviour we experience in this school?
- Do you feel adequately supported in dealing with behaviour in this school?
- Describe a behaviour situation in which things went well.
- Describe a behaviour situation in which things went badly.

PARENT AND CARER CONSULTATION

Communication is key within any community. Having parents and carers on board from the start can make a big difference if you are looking to make changes in your school in the near future. Much like staff input, the trickiest part is understanding the perspective of parents and carers who don't usually get involved. I work with many parents and carers who, for a myriad of reasons, have difficult relationships with school and education. It is part of our job in schools to bridge this gap – and we may need to get creative. Rob Archard, Assistant Head and Lead on Behaviour at a specialist SEMH school, says as a parent of three – "If a teacher understands my child, and I can see that – they can say anything! That's where I start with our pupils, you have to know them."

Please also be mindful of pupils who don't live with biological parents, are part of the care system or live in a children's home. They are all a part of your community. This needs to be recognised as possibly the 'why' around their behaviour and supported appropriately.

BEHAVIOUR AND REWARDS DATA

Yes, your behaviour and rewards data can give you the names of your repeat offenders, and the achievements or misdemeanours they are regularly involved in. Go deeper, ask questions:

- Is there a pattern to your data?
- Are a higher percentage of non-white pupils being punished for behaviour compared to the demographic landscape across the school? – Why?

- Which demographic is most likely to be excluded from your school?
- Are more girls receiving rewards than boys? Is there a point in which this stops? – Why?
- Are there specific times in the day, week or term that behaviour issues occur or rewards are given out? – Why?
- Are SEND pupils more likely to be punished than non-SEND pupils? – Why?
- Are children in care more likely to be punished for absences? – Why?
- What are your patterns regarding bullying? What type of pupils are most likely to be bullying? Is there a commonality of the pupils being bullied? – What education piece do you need to address here? – Homophobia? Islamophobia? Anti-foreigners?

Re-read Chapter 7 – find your and your school's biases. Even better, get an outside, neutral eye to do this. Analysing the data is the start – it's the education strategy you then apply that will shift the culture.

INCLUSION AND EQUALITY AUDIT

Extending from data analysis, you can carry out a school- or community-wide audit. This can become a huge job, so, as Dellenty (2010) suggests in his book *Celebrating Difference*, you can choose to approach a short, medium, or long term schedule depending on the factors that you wish to find out. Dellenty (2010) then gives a useful list of areas to consider in an audit considering LGBT+ inclusion (well worth a read). I have adapted his work here with a behaviour lens:

SHORT TERM
- Existing attitudes towards pupils with the most behavioural needs – amongst themselves, the staff and their peers.
- Existing attitudes towards the current behaviour policy and rules.
- Existing resources, models and images both at classroom level and schoolwide, that explicitly teach and model positive relationships, self-regulation, where to find support for wellbeing and positive mental health.

MEDIUM TERM
- Confidence of staff in the current approaches to behaviour and dealing with more extreme behaviour.
- Existing pastoral strategies for developing good emotional health, wellbeing and resilience.

LONG TERM
- Whether existing school vision, ethos, behaviour expectations, guidelines and policies are supportive with pupils with minority identities.
- Existing induction and staff training resources that are inclusive of supporting pupils with additional behavioural needs.

- Existing areas in the curriculum where contextuality of behaviour may be discussed, for example varying approaches to law and punishment in different parts of the world, with a comparison to your school and country.
- Protective factors and threats for those who have experienced trauma, abuse or neglect, have SEMH or are children in care, including pastoral support and links to outside agencies.
- Pupil, staff, parent, carer and governor needs and attitudes in terms of securing safe inclusion of those with additional behavioural needs and their families.
- Existing local and national knowledge around potential partnerships and collaborative working.
- Opportunities for celebrations outside of work undertaken in school regarding positive relationships, welcoming community and shared understanding and respect.
- The current diversity of role models and speakers invited to speak to your pupils.
- Existing strategies to ensure high-level accountability for all staff working with due regard to the core ethos of the Equality Act 2010.

INSPECTIONS

In much of Britain, schools must also work in line with the inspecting body framework. At different times the behaviour focus shifts, and of course you have to be mindful of this – there should be a governor and other teaching staff who ensure that your school is adhering.

In conversation with David Gumbrell, Head for over 20 years and senior lecturer for teacher training at Kingston University, we identified key ways to evidence where behaviour is working for external verification:

- Policies
- Letters (emails) from parents and carers
- Data and tracking
- Audits
- Peer reviews
- Attendance data

Essentially, gather evidence of longstanding progress, illustrate the bigger picture and trends, not the blips that may be seen on a one-off, high tension visit when all your staff are on hyper alert and, of course, the pupils' behaviour is affected.

NOW WHAT?

Going through these processes will inevitably give you ideas of the next steps you want to and need to take. Now, armed with all that knowledge, is a good time to study the behaviour policy, asking questions such as:

- Is it a good reflection of the issues we face in our school *now?*
- Does it provide practical, actionable steps?
- Are there areas missing?
- Who do I need support from to improve this?
- Where can I find inspiration for other approaches?
- What's the first thing to action?

You also need to consider the bigger picture; as former Headteacher George Gilchrist, now writer and speaker on Education and Leadership, advocates: if we only ever look at one area of school development at a time, the result is piecemeal and fragmented – only to be repeated in a cycle a few years down the line. Instead, he suggests an approach based on ecology:

> In ecology, it is understood how inter-connected all organisms and their physical environment are. Something having an impact on one organism, or piece of their environment, has impacts for others. When we look at individual eco-systems, we can identify relationships and interconnectivity which contribute to the wellness of the whole.
>
> If we were to adopt a similar approach in education, we would recognise that everything we do has impacts on the learners, and their learning, and we can't look at, or change, one aspect of our practice without seeing and thinking about impacts in every other area. (Gilchrist, 2020)

When it comes to behaviour I couldn't agree more.

A pupil becomes distracted when they aren't engaged in the lesson:

The lesson is interpreted as unengaging for them because their needs are not being met, or the pedagogical approach is unsuitable, or there's outside factors that create social, emotional, economical, practical, logistic barriers.

The reason for challenging behaviour in your school is multi-pronged. Hence why re-wording a behaviour policy alone will have little to no effect. Instead, you're looking for a culture shift – or as Gilchrist suggests, a change to the ecologic system of your community and environment.

Shifting or maintaining the culture around behaviour in any school cannot be done by one person, even if they are the leader on paper, as it requires a culture shift. These take time and they require others to be on board.

Whether it's a quick revision of the rewards procedure or a complete overhaul of the school's entire approach to behaviour, you need a diverse team around you made up of representatives of all of those it could affect – pupils (particularly ones known for behavioural issues), teachers, TAs, admin staff, parents, carers, governors etc. Consider the different minority characteristics you have in your school community and how these percentages compare to the people in your team.

Then give yourself a time frame with key evaluation points along the way.

From here, there are many ways you can approach this type of project, including Action Research methods, Practitioner Enquiry, visits and partnerships with other schools, sharing best practices around the borough etc. You must find the framework that works for you.

<u>Case Study: Barrowford Primary School –</u>
Learn to Love, Love to Learn

Barrowford Primary, in Lancashire, UK, is a two-form entry mainstream primary school with an exceptional, transformational journey around schoolwide approaches to behaviour. Headteacher there for 12 years, at the school for 14 years, Rachel Tomlinson explains:

> Our approach to 'behaviour' is very different; for lots of people when they say 'behaviour' they mean 'compliance' so when they talk about 'bad behaviour' they're talking about 'non-compliance' whereas when we talk about behaviour, we're thinking about what that might mean and how we can accommodate what that means because of what their behaviour is telling us.

On paper (or on website) this results in them working with a Relationship Management Policy, rather than a behaviour policy – available online, see below.

This wasn't where they began when Rachel started. The ethos she had inherited was a dictatorial and punitive approach to behaviour, that included a 'traffic light' reward and punishment system; the same pupils would win or lose (and get shouted at by the Head) at the end of each week, and staff had quotas of how many reward points they were able to give out per lesson. This lack of autonomy for staff was also reflected in the pedagogy and curriculum – as Rachel, on arrival, was handed a box of all her lessons plans day-by-day for the year.

As discussed, a behavioural culture change wouldn't occur overnight. Rachel's first move as Head was to let go of the 'traffic light' behaviour system that was being used alongside Golden Time as a punishment and bring in training around Attachment and Trauma – at the start three to four trainings a term, solely focusing on this area. Soon this enabled staff to bring in their own strategies for managing behaviour, based on the science and evidence they had learnt. Inevitably, there were some staff who moved on and felt this approach wasn't for them. As Gilchrist highlighted, the changes in one area were having an impact across the school. Trust was needed to know that the right team would form for this new approach to behaviour.

At the time, Lancashire Local Authority was offering free four-day training on Nurture Training (with Nurture UK) and Restorative Practice that Barrowford took advantage of. Initially it was a wake-up call, as Rachel explains:

We don't do any of this, what are we missing? So in my second year we set up a Nurture Group and started using Restorative Practices. That supplemented the strategies that the staff had developed for themselves.

They also worked closely with an LA Educational Psychologist who provided unofficial staff supervision once every half term. As new staff, on board with the new approach, came to replace the others, they hit a critical mass – and parents and carers started getting in contact to bring their children to the school from other schools: "we built up a record amongst parents that we could 'manage tricky behaviours.'" In the third year of Rachel's Headship the school moved fully to using a Relationships Policy, became completely no-sanctions and fully Restorative. Nowadays they offer that training in-house with their expertise. At this point they still used rewards in a big way across the whole school, as Rachel observes, at this time:

> we probably needed that to get our community onside and enabled parents to be a part of it, because they knew that we really loved their kids and wanted to celebrate them: we had two learning heroes from every class, Headteacher's award – based on a specific skill, dinner-time heroes, stickers, and we'd celebrate birthdays […] an hour every week was focused on celebration.

> We got to a point where we had 80–90% of our staff on board with Restorative Practice, by then we had a big pastoral team – we'd employed a counsellor and a Pastoral Manager […] there were all sorts of other things around that too: becoming Dyslexia friendly, Autism friendly, ADHD friendly and we made the school low sensory – turned the bell off, we started to eat in classrooms with the staff – we were trying to pinpoint the difficult times of the day, and dinnertimes is one of them – the most unstructured time of the day where you're putting your least qualified, your least experienced, your least paid members of staff in – why are you surprised that that's a flash point? So why are we doing that when we knew that we could support our children through – so we timetabled that. Dinnertimes and breaktimes are flexible – giving the teacher autonomy there. Lots of small stuff that was trying to stop the visual and actual noise around the school […] on the other side we had a really meaningful curriculum that really engaged the kids and gave them a voice.

(Continued)

Later they had another turning point, after visiting a local nursery school and watching the cringeworthy moment of 'Employee of the month' – which inspired them to ask their pupils about their experiences of all the reward assemblies and 'Student of the week' awards. As I have experienced myself with student consultations, when framed in the right way pupils nearly always step up to the responsibility being asked of them in this type of work and if staff are able to listen and believe, huge useful shifts can happen that wouldn't have otherwise. The student council's response was direct regarding rewards – "Well, we know you (the adults) like it [...] we know we all get a turn." Feeling stunned and patronised, they dug deeper, asking what pupils do want when they did really well, again a clear response – "for one of our special adults to know". That week they scrapped the rewards emphasis and re-focused on community time – in assemblies, a pupil reporting back on everyone's learning from the class that week. They get as many parents and carers, if not more, attending now.

Whilst interviewing Rachel about schoolwide behaviour, I was struck by how few times she said the word. To sum it up she explains: "rather than seeing it as the child's job to come and behave in school, we see it as our job to make our context a context in which it is easy for them to be successful." I am honoured to have been supporting the school with their most recent addition – the creation of a new SEMH unit within the mainstream school.

http://barrowford.lancs.sch.uk/

Case Study: Bukky Yusuf: Senior Leader – Mainstream to Special School

Bukky Yusuf is a senior leader, science teacher, coach and ambassador for Leadership Matters. She has undertaken a number of leadership roles within the mainstream, working for over 20 years in various schools; more recently she has transferred her skills over to special schools. Bukky is a Network Leader and coach for WomenEd and BAMEEd. She also champions the wellbeing of educators through the #Teacher5ADay initiative and is widely involved in the EdTech world.

She is currently a part time Senior Leader in a Special school for 14–19 year olds. There are around twenty pupils in the school, all of whom have not been in a school setting for at least six months prior to attending the school.

Bukky begins with a key question regarding schoolwide approaches to behaviour. As I outlined above, she starts with the individual pupils: "If a child has behaviour needs, what is that telling you about their learning needs?" In comparison to mainstream SEND support – which often gave teachers generic strategies for learning needs – Bukky has found in special schools that you have to be much more specific. Echoing that, when the behavioural needs are bigger, there's a greater need for investigating exactly what's needed through consultations, audits, surveys etc.

After reading an IEP (Individual Education Plan) Bukky sensitively asks the pupil "What does this mean? How can I help you to learn in ways that work best for you?" From that place, when organising schoolwide CPD it is based on what the pupils need now – an ongoing exploration that ensures that our 'behaviour work' will never be done. Part of that, she feels, is creating experiential learning for staff that hits home on what it's like to have the needs the pupils have, for example: "As a neurotypical person, we may not really understand what it means to be neurodiverse. We need to put ourselves in this position of understanding." She advocates strongly that special schools need the best teachers to do this, alongside a behaviour policy that is consistent and yet flexible: "We understand that one size does not fit all." There are no behaviour points at her school. When there is an incident, there is a follow up and the incident is logged.

Alongside this, every Wednesday after school, staff meet to discuss the needs of the pupils, reflecting on their data: pen portrait (a passport of needs and skills of each child), EHCP and IEP. They consider the triggers, the behaviour and any trauma a child has experienced – this discussion leads to questions such as "What does this mean for our approaches to behaviour? Do we need to put specific structures in place to support this pupil?" – which become points of differentiation and action. If a pupil is having difficulty learning, Bukky sees it as the school's job to create support systems or spaces that help pupils regulate, so they are ready to learn, she emphasises: "This is not a reward, it is a recognition of their needs. If their behaviour shows that something is off balance, some of them will really struggle to access the work themselves." Bukky advocates sessions like this for staff to work together to discuss the children: "Not a whinge session, but a chance to ask what could help the child and the whole school in terms of learning?"

When a pupil first attends the school there is a wraparound assessment process: there is an initial assessment, in the form of a conversation with the pupil and practical assessments that show how the curriculum might work for the child, how they might respond to different settings, different learning needs they may have, and subject specific tests. These pupils are not just data.

(Continued)

Asked about schoolwide approaches to behaviour, Bukky recalls one main-stream school that gave her a very unfortunate example of when it goes wrong, "The behaviour system was too complex! I was not clear what to do, the behaviour system divided the senior team." In an experienced point in her career, Bukky recalls feeling like she couldn't teach – because there was no coherence across the school's culture, "it didn't feel safe". This emphasises the point that behaviour cannot be shifted by one person, it will take the majority of a community to shift a culture, as Bukky experienced above.

Bukky advises:

> The whole staff need to look at what the issues are, senior leaders and middle leaders. They need to listen – how are they helping? How are they not? What are they not aware of? Create open and honest questionnaires. It can be useful to use an external organisation for this, so that the process is completely transparent.

> Any behaviour policy has to work with the students you have got. You need to understand the heartbeat of your school [...] SLT need to be consistently slow *and* quick; don't throw everything at it. When you start at a new school, get to know the school community *first* [...] You need to constantly review, build in review periods – for teachers, pupils, SLT – fine tune your systems to make them work.

As final advice to senior leaders on behaviour, Bukky cheerleads:

> believe in yourself, when you get advice about issues with behaviour systems, don't internalise it. Take it as information that highlights some things that need to be tweaked. We need to think of ourselves as learners – we all come to school.

Action Box

Next lesson

Plan your day to follow a pupil around your school. Wipe everything else off the diary!

Next week

Meet with: some pupils, some TAs, some dinner supervisors, some teachers, other leaders, parents, governors (or when in meetings with them already), and start asking the questions you need to know about their experiences of behaviour in your school – and listen.

Long term

Go through the audit suggested here, or search for frameworks or external behaviour consultants who can help you with the culture of behaviour in your school so that *all* of your pupils have a context in which they can learn.

What has any of this got to do with behaviour?

The schoolwide culture towards behaviour will directly impact the job the teaching staff can do and the learning that can take place with your young people – especially those with the most extreme behaviour needs. If we are willing to explore the behaviour culture in an inclusive way, as suggested in this chapter, we can prevent many an exclusion and children ending up as a negative statistic on the outskirts of society.

Further reading

Celebrating Difference: A Whole-School Approch to LGBT+ Inclusion – Shaun Dellenty (2010)

I had been waiting for this book for years. A guide for schools to make organisational change to LGBT+ inclusion. It provides a detailed six-tier approach on shifting the culture of a school.

School Leadership – A Scottish Perspective – George Gilchrist

With the benefit of a number of Head roles in his career, George offers a personal perspective on leadership, understanding that we will continue to improve our education systems and schools by sharing our best practice. http://scotedublogs.org/author/george-gilchrist/ (accessed March 26, 2021).

(Continued)

Behaviour in School: Relationship Management Policy – Barrowford School

The Relationship Policy developed and used effectively at Barrowford School, where Rachel is the Headteacher. http://barrowford.lancs.sch.uk/wp-content/uploads/2020/02/Behaviour-in-schools.pdf (accessed March 26, 2021).

Nurture UK

A UK wide organisation dedicated to removing barriers to learning through providing mental health support for pupils. The website provides research and evidence on practice and shares strategies as to how this can help in schools. www.nurtureuk.org/ (accessed March 26, 2021).

Whole School Approach to SEMH – Adele Bates

https://adelebateseducation.co.uk/whole-school-approach-to-semh/ (accessed March 26, 2021).

Differentiation for Pupils with SEMH – Adele Bates

https://adelebateseducation.co.uk/differentiation-for-pupils-with-semh/ (accessed March 26, 2021).

Blog posts sharing specific startegies for supporting SEMH pupils.

10

"MISS, DO YOU ACTUALLY KNOW WHAT YOU'RE DOING?": TROUBLESHOOTING

#INSULTOFTHEWEEK

"Miss, can you please stop breathing? It's putting me off my work."

IN THIS CHAPTER YOU WILL

- Get quick advice and signposting on solving common behaviour issues.

INTRODUCTION

You feel like you've tried everything and it's still not working?

This chapter is a quick-fire-round on potentially troubleshooting topics. Skip to the topics you need immediate help with.

"AH! I STARTED ALL WRONG WITH A PUPIL OR CLASS – HOW CAN I GET THEM BACK?"

If ever you want to change a relationship or a culture you have to go back to basics. In addition, you may need to be honest. If genuine, honesty can be powerful. I once started on the wrong foot with a girl in my class, there was an underlying tit-for-tat competitiveness going on, one that didn't feel like a healthy teacher-pupil relationship. I reflected and realised that this girl reminded me of a girl when I was at school who used to tease me. I was still playing the same game, only the responses had transferred to another girl – oh, and I was now also her adult teacher, not her classmate. It took some unpicking, but once I realised this, I was able to move forwards. I had a one-to-one discussion with her, of course it would have been inappropriate to tell her my school-life history. I did say, "I feel we've got off on the wrong foot, and I'm sorry about that. I would love to start again because I can see that you're very capable in my subject. Even if you don't like me, I wouldn't want that to get in the way of your learning. How does that sound? Is there anything I can do to make that easier for you?" I started looking for her positives – of which there were many, it's just I hadn't been able to see them because I was *expecting* not to see them. This can be done with a class too. If you've reached loggerheads where every lesson is a battle, you're likely to have slipped into some variation of the nagging-tone (any gender can fall into this one, I have evidence). To start turning a relationship around, you need to start convincing first yourself, and then the class, that it is possible. See the next 'Check back' box for more.

"AH! THEY WON'T STAY QUIET"

This is an extension of starting out wrongly, a boundaries and expectations issue. Until you can nip this one in the bud, it will continually return. It is worth putting the leg work in. I once had a Year 9 class who I had lost, I couldn't give any instruction without interruptions. I ended up spending three weeks' worth of lessons re-establishing boundaries. Yes, it will be painful, and seemingly you won't be 'teaching.' But it works. After those three weeks, when the class knew I meant business, they ended up being one of the best classes to teach – focused, engaged and willing to learn.

CHECK BACK TO

- Chapter 1 – Boundaries
- Chapter 2 – The three non-negotiables

"AH! THEY WON'T SIT STILL"

They've got ants in their pants, and it's not always from Early Years. It's worth checking what lesson or activity they have before yours. I once made a mistake that gave a colleague of mine much more work. As a treat in English, I led drama sessions on a Friday fourth period with a class. Friday period five they had Maths. Unbeknownst to me, I was sending the pupils to him with the 'end of week feel-good vibe' that was not conducive to focusing on his Pythagoras. The Maths Teacher investigated what was causing the raucous joviality and contacted me. He explained the situation and asked if I might 'calm them down a bit' before they got to him. He was completely right to do so, I built in a five-minute 'cool down' to the lesson, which then enabled them to focus in Maths. If the reason for the wandering wonders is something out of your control, then you need to put in a 'ready to learn' activity into the start of your lesson. I always return to free writing. In addition, particularly if it's a double lesson, put in a physical break within your lesson. It can still be related to the theme, but put an activity within your planning that gets them up on their feet and using their excess energy to your advantage. If it is only one or two pupils, be sure to always have a couple of urgent errands handy. If you don't have any, send them to a friendly colleague with a (closed) note "Fatima needed a walk". With some pupils I'm completely open and say to them, "I can see you need to stretch your legs, if I give you an 'errand' for five minutes to get some fresh air, will you come back and concentrate for the rest of the lesson?" It works well for fairly trustworthy pupils who need a little help self-regulating. The rest of the time, ensure you communicate clear expectations and boundaries around remaining seated. See "Ah! I can't get silence" section for further ideas.

CHECK BACK TO

- Chapter 3 – Free writing
- Chapter 2 – Routines and consistency

"AH! I'M GETTING INTO ARGUMENTS"

This suggests that something the pupils are saying is triggering you personally. You are the adult, you need to reflect on what this is about, if you can in the moment. Sometimes, it's best to pass on to a colleague if you know a certain topic is going to trigger you. For the unavoidable times, experiment with not responding or retaliating (it won't be easy). "We will have a chat about this at break" is a great way to give you both time to cool down. Maybe at break a trusted colleague is invited in to facilitate the discussion. Longer term, this is something that you need to take time to find the root of. Pupils will occasionally trigger us because we are human, but if this is a recurring pattern then reach out to a mentor, supervisor or counsellor who can support you.

CHECK BACK TO

- Chapter 4 – See behaviour as communication and negotiate
- Chapter 4 – Interview with Frédérique Lambrakis-Haddad
- Chapter 6 – Teenage brains

"AH! THEY KEEP WALKING OUT OF THE CLASSROOM"

It is a bit trickier to teach from there, isn't it? You can also feel helpless and humiliated in front of the other pupils. In the moment, let them go. It can feel counterintuitive, but you have another thirty-one pupils in front of you who do need your attention and if you do the follow up later then it will work. The second piece of action is to let someone know as soon as possible, so that you do not have an absence or safety issue on your hands. Email, call or reach out to a colleague as soon as you can. All you need to say is "Ella has left my classroom, I'm going to continue to teach the rest."

But the real solution is in the follow up.

If a human needs to exit a space, against established social etiquette, then there is a reason. What is the trigger? What is going on behind this behaviour? What are they getting away from, or going towards (in one school at which I worked, this conversation led me to finding out about lesson time smoking meet ups in the toilets...)? Once you know those answers, then you can deal with strategies to keep them in. This may take time; you will need to have discussions with the pupil outside of the lesson time. Ask a trusted colleague to facilitate if you feel you might struggle. The key is persistence. Every time they walk out of your classroom you need to have a follow up conversation, ideally later in the day, or at the latest the following day. That way they know they can't get away with it. See the next 'Check back' box for more.

"A PUPIL SCREAMS IN MY CLASS FOR A REACTION"

Similar to above, there is a reason for this behaviour and until you find out what it is, it will be hard to reduce and stop it. If at all possible, do not react in the moment. Follow the steps as suggested in the "Ah! They keep walking out of the classroom!" section.

CHECK BACK TO

- Chapter 2 – Routines and consistency and trauma informed practice
- Chapter 3 – Connection before correction and PACE

"AH! MY ASC/ADHD PUPIL IS ALLOWED TO GET AWAY WITH THINGS THE OTHERS AREN'T!"

There is not a quick fix for this one. For any pupil who has different needs to others, it also demonstrates clearly why differentiation is so important – we are all different. For some it will play out more obviously than others. The reason is because we live in a society that is based not on neurodiversity. We live in an ableist society. To change the culture in your classroom, to include pupils who happen to be outside of the majority, will take your effort and dedication to the idea that equality does not mean the same.

The best thing to do is get as much information as possible. Aside from the label, what else do you know about this pupil? Start from a pedagogical perspective – where are their learning skills? For which subjects or tasks do they have a natural flair? What style of learning do they engage with best? Consider the learning environment. One Autistic pupil and I worked out that the reason for her not being able to work in a certain classroom once a week was because of the next door's class cooking. That smell, for her heightened senses, was too much and my adult senses, weakening with age, could not detect the smell in the same way. With this information, consider if the way you have presented your expectations in the room are accessible to the pupil. If you realise they can only take in one instruction at a time, is that how you deliver them – every time? How can you differentiate expectations and boundaries in a way that they understand and is achievable for them? How will you know that they have understood? For example, a pupil with ADHD and a short attention span is unlikely to sit through your sixty-minute lesson, no matter how hard they try. They will need your help to do so – yes, you will have to differentiate for them. Look at your relationship – have you built upon it? Can they trust you? What's something you have in common? Essentially, all the usual approaches apply, but it will require more persistence. Seek extra support from the team around the child and extra training.

CHECK BACK TO

- Chapter 2 – Routines and consistency and when rules go wrong
- Chapter 4 – Check in regularly
- Chapter 7 – Bias and unconscious bias

"AH! MY PUPILS ARE WINDING EACH OTHER UP AND FIGHTING WITH EACH OTHER!"

Think back to the teenage brain information in Chapter 6. We know at this time that peer endorsement is more important than adults' approval *in the brain* of the teen. Winding each other up and fighting are signs of pupils not feeling comfortable, feeling threatened by one another and/or the situation they are in. Knowing that, you need to get to the bottom of it, if it is going to stop disrupting your lessons. Do this individually. There is no point addressing the whole class on it: in front of you they may comply, but we know that when they are feeling threatened, heightened emotions will arise, and your well-meaning talk will be long forgotten. Pick two pupils to begin with – the main players are a good place to start. Form relationships with them *outside* of your classroom, and not all about your lessons either. Observe them in other lessons you know they get on well in and learn. Learn about what it is that is causing the behaviour in your lessons, ask others, find out what's going on at home. Like many of these things, when it comes back to behaviour, unless you know *why,* even with punishment you will only ever be fostering temporary compliance – that does not solve the issue. If the issue is serious (I have discovered long-running family feuds, and cultural and religious ongoing conflict at some roots) then it might be that you need to physically separate certain pupils whilst you are still investigating. Call in departmental support on how you might arrange this. Once you have some ideas about what the main problems are, then you can facilitate restoration. Remember, pupils (even big ones) are still children and still learning, they may need prompting and help to work out how to get on with others. Use a framework for conflict such as Restorative Practice or Non-Violent Conflict. Imagine if every pupil left your school knowing how to make peace with others, despite differences, imagine how different the world would be – you're teaching them a golden skill for life (which could prevent wars).

CHECK BACK TO

- Chapter 3 – PACE
- Chapter 6 – Teenage brains

"A PUPIL HAS TARGETED ME (GOOD OR BAD)"

This can be tricky and is another example of how even as teaching staff, we are also human. Most importantly, remember that you are the adult. There will be reasons that the pupil has either taken to you or seems to have a vendetta against you – most of the time, this is nothing to do with you *personally.* However, it feels personal because something about the situation is triggering for you. It may be as simple as, it's the end of term, you're tired and a pupil finds your Achilles heel – never to let it go.

Step away, remember you are the adult, and reflect on the pattern that might be happening here. Has this happened before? When was the first time you remember someone treating you in this way in your life? How is this the same and different? Find a trusted colleague to discuss this with, which will lead you to the answers of how to continue the relationship more appropriately.

CHECK BACK TO

- Chapter 4 – Interview with Frédérique Lambrakis-Haddad
- Chapter 6 – Teenage brains and still not convinced that things aren't personal?

"AH! MY PUPILS CAN'T CONCENTRATE"

Approach this from a teaching and learning perspective first, rather than a behaviour one. What is it about the style of learning that is not meeting the pupils' needs? Do they need more interaction? Shorter instructions? Shorter tasks and small recognitions of achievement throughout a lesson? Mini breaks within your lesson? Sensory breaks? A stretch and a look at some nature out of the window? Are there specific SEND or EAL needs that are not being met? Are there outside influences that are affecting their concentration? Ask other colleagues about their experiences of the class or pupils. Is it something about your lessons that is not engaging them or is there something across school that needs addressing? Find out the why and you can experiment with different strategies to address it.

CHECK BACK TO

- Chapter 4 – Behaviour as communication and in the classroom
- Chapter 7 – Introduction and emotional labour

"AH! I ONLY WORK WITH A CLASS ONCE A WEEK OR FORTNIGHT AND I CAN'T ESTABLISH BOUNDARIES"

I made a huge mistake with this scenario a few years back. I taught a Year 7 class once a fortnight for their 'Library session' – it wasn't even a proper lesson. So I rocked up fun and jovial throughout, thinking little of establishing relationships or boundaries. A dire approach that I regretted for a full two years afterwards – especially for Year 7 who are only just learning about the culture of a school. The pupils needed the boundaries, they still needed to feel safe and guided by high expectations. Unlike my Year 11s who I'd worked with for two years, they didn't know what my unspoken-every-lesson-expectations were, and I treated them as if they did, then wondered why they ran across the library sometimes pretending to be cars in a Formula One race. I just about held it together for the year. With a sigh of relief, I waved them goodbye in the summer, only to receive my September timetable and of course, find the very same class on my regular

English teaching slots as Year 8s. It took *a lot* of work to prove to them that I was a 'real teacher' and not a library monitor.

So, don't do what I did. Instead, put the same amount of time into explicitly teaching and discussing expectations and building initial relationships as you would any other class, whilst realising there's some maths that has to play out here: if you see one class three times a week, it might take six weeks to feel that you have established the classroom culture and begun some positive relationships within the classroom – that process has taken you eighteen lessons, plus the marking, planning and follow up work in between seeing them. If you only see a class for one lesson a fortnight, the same process will take 36 weeks – and that's without a curriculum down day or emergency sports trip taking a few lessons off the list; in reality it will most likely take longer. If you see them so rarely, you are less likely to be devoting as much energy to them. In my case, the library sessions required very little planning, and there was no marking, and so my actual amount of time spent thinking about these pupils was small. When the behaviour issues started arising, I also found myself trying to consciously think about them *less* as they were the only class who didn't seem to want to conform to my wannabe-Mary-Poppins-style-wonder. So, with all that rough maths in mind, theoretically it would take you over a year to establish the same kind of rapport that you would with your other three times a week classes.

So the solutions? Number one, don't judge yourself too harshly. Now you know the maths, you can see that it would, in fact, be *strange* if your relationship with this class were better than your others. Annoyingly of course the two play out simultaneously, so whilst your other classes' relationships are progressing well, this one you're still on the basics. Being aware of this helps stop comparisons. Moreover, you need to invest that time and energy, when you can, into focusing on this class. My solution was to ask a trusted colleague to observe me. It was hard – my ego wanted her to watch the classes that were working, but that wouldn't have helped. Getting another teacher's perspective can massively help you see the holes that you undoubtedly are missing. Another useful tactic is to find out expectations of their usual class teacher. It may feel odd, but it can be a quick trick for an easier run of it to start with. So for example, if the main teacher asks them to line up outside the classroom before entering, or she insists on tucked in shirts before entering, or the starter is done in silence, do the same. Take some time to observe them working in their other established lessons. I am not suggesting you emulate other teachers' entire persona – that doesn't work, but the actions can be the same, which will help pupils fall back on something they *are* used to more than once a fortnight.

CHECK BACK TO

- Chapter 2 – The three non-negotiables
- Chapter 3 – First impressions

"AH! I CAN'T GET SILENCE"

Before we go onto the pupils, think first about yourself. Can you maintain silence when stood next to your friends? Remember, it is a skill that needs developing. Some of us can feel very awkward in silence, nervous and anxious even, and there are those of us who will rush to fill it. It is a skill, and it's one you can help your pupils develop, if you have it yourself first.

This issue about pupils not respecting silence is usually a symptom of not maintaining that silence in the past. The problem is many teachers ask for 'silence' when what they really mean is 'quiet working with the odd bit of chat'. So, in your classroom, when you ask for silence you need to show them what you mean by that. The trick with this one is that you have to wait for it, and in the waiting it can feel like years, and so it's hard to hold, and we give in to some inane brain chatter telling us "but they should be learning, what about the curriculum, you've got to finish the topic by half term, if someone walked in now they would think I am out of control" and so on. Ignore it. This is a test of your boundaries. I can say that on more than one occasion I have waited for more than twenty minutes for silence – but only ever once with any class. Then they get it. You can experiment with different activities you do whilst you're waiting for silence: many teachers revert to the *hard-and-scary-stare* or worse, shouting – which totally defeats the object of silence, and does not role model your request. In fact, you are then holding pupils to expectations you can't keep yourself. The absolute number one best tactic I have found over the years is the *disinterested or bored* approach. You don't need to repeat the instruction, they know it – and that most likely leads to the shouting. Instead, physically stay present in a prominent place where everyone can see you and then look out of the window, look bored (I sometimes exaggerate it into 'bored teen body language' – if that works for you). On more than one occasion I have even been known to walk over to my desk, grab a chair and my bag, move back to the centre front point and do my knitting. Frequently I look up, I retain eye contact with individuals and either smile if they are maintaining silence, or if not give a bit of a mimed sign. Meanwhile *not on the board* you can make a note of those who will need to stay behind for wasting your time. If you put it on the board you are provoking reactions – they will not be silent ones. Don't do it.

I am not a fan of whole class punishments – I remember the injustice of it when I was at school. Instead, at the end of the lesson you simply say: "if I call your name out, remain seated, everyone else can go." If, like me, you insist on silence at the end of the lesson before leaving then you can work this another way; if you catch the eyes of someone who has followed the instruction, you smile, thank them for their time and let them know they can go. At first the noisy ones won't notice, but bit by bit they will, guaranteed to be answered by "How come they get to go?! *That's not fair.*" At which point you simply state (I sometimes do this with a touch of mock surprise) "Oh, they followed the instruction." The whole point is, they have to hit your expectation if they want to go.

Now, let's go to the next important question around silence: *why* are you requesting it?

Sometimes silence is genuinely helpful – mock exams spring to mind. Other times it is helpful for some of your pupils to be able to concentrate. However, if you think that silence is a symbol of control or even learning then you're wrong. A forced silence is a symbol of compliance – compliance does not mean anyone is learning anything, apart from maybe resentment. Pupils over the years have mastered the 'silence-and-working-hard-look' only for teachers around the globe to look at the work at the end of the lesson to find doodles, usually of male genitalia. So why *would* you use silence?

- To help pupils concentrate
- To think
- To reflect
- To listen
- For an exam
- For holding two-minute national silences
- As a 'ready for learning' at the beginning or 'cool down' at the end of a class

A pupil once stayed after a lesson to ask me, quite rightly, why I had my rule about silence, standing behind chairs with shirts tucked in at the end of every lesson. He told me it was stupid and dictatorial. I agreed with him, it was completely arbitrary, and then I explained: I need to hold a safe classroom in which sometimes I will give instructions that need to be followed, they could range from how to use equipment safely to how to not fail question four on paper two of the GCSE exam. I needed to support a culture in my classroom in which, whilst we are all equal human beings, my role in that classroom is slightly different to theirs – it is to guide. The three particular non-negotiables I'd chosen could really have been anything, but what they did was practice the status in our relationship. If I were working with a class who couldn't manage simple tasks like that, how could I deliver more complicated instructions?

Equally, in my classrooms we were often known to act out big dramatic battle scenes that may have involved much shouting, climbing on desks, using chairs as weapons and human pyramids whilst acting out, for example, a Capulet vs Montague brawl. I explained to the pupil that I could only 'allow' them freedom to do that, if I knew that on my instruction, they would be able to return to other types of learning, tidy up or, if things were getting out of hand, I could reign them back in for everyone's safety. I said that I felt these three requests at the end of the lesson were quite easy tasks, and moreover they complimented the school's behaviour and uniform policy – so none of my managers questioned me. It was not that I particularly agreed with them – I find shirts in or out rarely affect a person's ability to analyse non-fiction texts, but it was useful for our class to fit in with the expectations of the school at large.

Also, I explained, because our lessons were often lively, it was important that I also gave all of us some time to transition into whatever activities were to follow. Silence is a good method of reflecting, breathing and thinking about how we might approach the next part of our day. The silence was a *tool* to support learning. The pupil confirmed "So your instructions about chairs and shirts could be anything, you could be asking us to hop on one leg until we can go, but the silence helps us come down a bit." "Yes," I replied. He was satisfied.

For yourself, starting with the aim of having whole lessons in silence is a big ask. For anyone. So pepper moments of silence when they are actually useful. Sometimes you can even ask a class, "We have ten minutes until break time, you need to finish question three or you stay behind, who would prefer silence to focus?" Take a vote.

As any composer will tell you, when used sparingly and in juxtaposition to noise, silence can be powerful. There is only one composer I know of who attempted to write an entire composition based on silence – and he very much proved that it was impossible. I doubt 10TR on a Tuesday after a wet play will disprove him. (John Cage's "4:33".)

CHECK BACK TO

- Chapter 2 – The three non-negotiables and when rules don't work
- Chapter 5 – Interview with Kate McAllister

"AH! I DON'T AGREE WITH MY SCHOOL'S BEHAVIOUR POLICY!"

Within reason, the most important aspect to supporting challenging behaviour in your classroom is that it works for you and your pupils. However, in some schools teachers are trusted less and have to 'prove' that they are toeing the party line. In my experience, if there are no complaints from your class you are unlikely to be questioned. However, if you approach behaviour in a very different way to the rest of the school this may also be challenging for the pupils as the difference in expectations is too wide.

There are two things you can do – one, is that you carry on with what you're doing *if it's working* and let the proof be in the pudding. When colleagues question you, you can show how you effectively manage behaviour, you don't need to pass judgement on how they do theirs. Useful common topics are boundaries and routines, as discussed in previous chapters. On the other hand, if it really does feel too different from your core values about working with young people, then it is worth considering option two: other settings. I know many a teacher who found that a switch of schools made all the difference to their wellbeing – mainly because they weren't having to fight upstream against a regime they didn't believe in. Teaching can be challenging enough, we don't have to make it harder. There is a school for you out there.

CHECK BACK TO

- Chapter 8 – Introduction and interview with Dr Emma Kell
- Chapter 9 – Case study with Bukky Yusuf

"AH! MY HOD SAYS I NEED TO BE MORE DISCIPLINED (OR 'DON'T SMILE BEFORE CHRISTMAS')!"

This may be useful, if not a little clumsy, feedback. Or it might be a variation of a clash in ideologies around supporting behaviour. You need to consider which one it might be, and definitely get a second opinion. It is rarely given as feedback, however, if classes are going well. So it does suggest that something is amiss. When people say that a teacher needs to be 'more disciplined' what they usually mean is that they are not holding boundaries. Unfortunately, this can often then be interpreted as needing to be more shouty, or demand silence more often or adopt a 'zero tolerance attitude' to bad behaviour. None of these will work for you if that is not who you are. Instead, you need to return to your own sense of boundaries. Take time to think and discuss with others, what is the kind of culture you want to foster in your classroom? Are there people in the school you can learn from to explore this topic further? If the answers leave you wanting to feel more confident in yourself, then you could do that. If, on the other hand, the answers lead you to values very different from your school's then see the "I don't agree with my school's behaviour policy" section. Smiling before Christmas, Hanukkah or Chinese New Year is totally up to you and what works for who you are as a teacher – remember, pupils smell inauthenticity a mile off.

CHECK BACK TO

- Chapter 1 – Boundaries and boundaries again
- Chapter 3 – First impressions and identity
- Chapter 8 – Interview with Dr Emma Kell

"AH! I DON'T HAVE ANY SUPPORT!"

This is similar to the trouble above. All teaching staff need support, whatever their role. If you're feeling isolated, then please reach out.

CHECK BACK TO

- Chapter 8 – Colleagues and interview with Dr Emma Kell

"AH! I'M SO NERVOUS ABOUT SCHOOL I CAN'T SLEEP!"

Ugh, I'm sorry. This is tough. Occasionally it happens to everyone, but if it is becoming a regular pattern then this is a sign that things are getting out of balance. You need support. *Please* ask for it. This pattern is not sustainable.

> ## CHECK BACK TO
>
> - Chapter 1 – Energy
> - Chapter 8 – Colleagues and interview with Dr Emma Kell

"AH! I CAN'T TEACH, I WANT TO QUIT!"

This is a hideous feeling to have. We have all been there, more than once, and just because we're very experienced, doesn't mean that it goes away. Every person's situation is different, and I can't answer that trouble without knowing about your situation. So I ask: please talk to someone, please find support *before* making any decisions.

What has any of this got to do with behaviour?

There are always troubles to shoot. There is no silver bullet. Regularly when I have a behaviour challenge I will ask a colleague for help, do research, and I've even been known to read my own resources for reminders!

The great thing is that you're here and learning.

CONCLUSION: "MISS, CAN I GO NOW?"

#INSULTOFTHEWEEK

Pupil: "Miss, you know we call you 'Miss Lates' for your nickname."

Me: "Good use of rhyme, why do you call me that?"

Pupil: "You give motivational speeches at the end of lessons and never let us out on time."

Me: "Oh well, there are worse teacher nicknames than that."

My vision for education is one in which all differences are included and welcomed; an education which is flexible, relevant and leads towards positive social change.

At the beginning of this book, I invited you to connect to a wider vision of what education could be for all. I hope it has sparked some ideas about how that could look both in your classroom and on a wider scale when it comes to supporting our young people with behavioural needs.

Much of the physical writing of this book happened during many on–off lockdowns of 2020. This year sent education, and everything else, into a complete whirl, with a devastating impact on so many. I'm sure there are many books now written on the matter.

The bit that interests me, though, outside of just the hideousness and surviving – is the questions that we can no longer ignore:

What is education for?

Who benefits from the current system? Who does not?

How are different needs accounted for?

Whose responsibility is it to educate our children?

To what extent should parents, carers or the government decide what is best for our children?

How important are exams? Who gains from them?

How are pupils affected when the experience of human connection is taken out of education?

What *is* more important – learning resilience and self-regulation in adverse conditions – or academic learning? Can the two coincide?

What makes us feel safe and happy, and is it possible that *this* is the key to learning?

During this time, I was interviewed on a panel with Lucy Emmerson from the Sex Education Forum. We were discussing the then delayed compulsory Relationship, Sex and Health Education curriculum that had originally been scheduled to take effect in schools that September. Before the interview I felt despondent, who would want to hear about how to teach puberty to SEMH pupils in a now delayed new curriculum? There were much more pressing issues to deal with: pupils not being able to access laptops and therefore teachers, parents and carers having to decide whether to fuel the heating or the computer with the coin top up electricity meter and for some children, not being able to access food as the government decided not to feed those on Free School Meals during 'holiday' times.

Luckily the host, Pete Henshaw, addressed the context directly, we were not ignoring a global pandemic for the sake of curriculum content. This freed us up to discuss what positive moves were being made, despite everything. Lucy brought up a point that, although I had experienced it, I had not articulated in my mind. A thought that has given me motivation and even excitement for our education system – and particularly for those with behavioural needs.

Lucy pointed out that discussions around mental health and wellbeing were being addressed in schools and society at large in a way that has never been done before. Checking in with someone and declaring "actually, I'm having a tough lockdown day" had become commonplace, and further than that – accepted. Lucy's point was: what better foundation could we have for an RSHE curriculum than that? One that begins with the focus on our mental health and wellbeing? (Henshaw, 2020).

I take this one step further:

A basis of shared vocabulary, awareness and acceptance of mental health and wellbeing – what better foundation could we have for an entire education system than that? So many of the strategies that I know that work for young people with behavioural needs (and can help others too) are based on this approach.

My cogs start to whirl when I connect with my own vision for education; if we have a shared basis of understanding of the differing and yet connected human experience at any one time, then we are on our way to inclusion. People's differences do not need to merely be tolerated but accepted and integrated into the astounding and fruitful collision of different people bringing their gifts together in co-creation to make positive social and environmental change.

Then we can welcome all difference into the education system, not as a bolt on intervention, but as part of the fabric of the whole approach. Once we admit that all our pupils are different, we begin to create systems that don't just account for or support difference in a 'high ability vs. low ability' strategy, but actually create space for difference to thrive, for acceptance of difference in individuals to be an asset to the school community as a whole. *This* is my vision for young people whose behaviour challenges the adults around them and the education system at large.

That's big, it can be overwhelming, and I can't do it on my own. So I use a similar structure that I have offered you in this book:

"What can I do next lesson for our young people with behavioural needs?"

For me, next lesson (or article, or panel discussion, or workshop, or keynote) I start with Chapter 1's guidelines: I look after myself first. That way, the contributions I make are the best they can possibly be, for the distressed young person hurling abuse in frustration of their own shame, or for the despairing school leader who needs a safe space to vent and some motivation to keep doing the best they can. I am human, it doesn't happen all the time, but I strive where I can to give my best attention to the small task in hand today, now.

"What can I do next week for our young people with behavioural needs?"

The idea of next week for me often involves collaboration. Connecting with likeminded educators or being educated by my pupils so that I am constantly being questioned, challenged, inspired and finding out where I'm making mistakes, where my holes in learning are and what I can do to improve them. I also love a good natter. I have been deeply inspired recently by the work of adrienne maree brown who advocates that enjoyment is key in the quest for change (brown, 2019), I'm playing with that.

"What can I do long term for our young people with behavioural needs?"

Create platforms, build bridges and generally bang my drum.

This story of behavioural challenges, learning needs, exclusion and societal judgement is not my educational story. On the contrary, the education system worked very well for pupils like me, with the type of childhood I had, in the time and place I had it. This is a privilege, and I choose to use that privilege to create opportunities. Opportunities for connection between 'us' and 'other', and opportunities for unheard stories of lived experience to be shared, in order to better inform how we build human society's infrastructures in a way that prevent us from killing each other and our planet.

What about you?

Thank you for playing along with me in this book. Now this is your homework, connect with me, let me know how you get on:

"What can you do next lesson, next week, long term to help our young people with behavioural needs?"

LIST OF ACRONYMS

Common acronyms used in this book and in the world of teaching young people with behavioural needs.

ACEs – Adverse Childhood Experiences

ADHD – Attention Deficit Hyperactivity Disorder

AP – Alternative Provision

ASC – Autistic Spectrum Condition

EBD – Emotional, Behavioural Difficulties

EHCP – Educational Health Care Plan

EP – Educational Psychologist

HLTA –Higher Level Teaching Assistant

HOD – Head of Department

IEP – Individual Education Plan

LA – Local Authority

LAC – Looked After Child

LSA – Learning Support Assistant

PRU – Pupil Referral Unit

SEMH – Social, Emotional, Mental Health Needs

SEND – Special Educational Needs and Disabilities

TA – Teaching Assistant

REFERENCES

Adebisi, F.I. (2019) 'The only accurate part of BAME is the "and"', *Foluke's African Skies*, July 8. https://folukeafrica.com/the-only-acceptable-part-of-bame-is-the-and/ (accessed March 26, 2021).

Ahlberg, A. (1984) 'The Supply Teacher' [poem], in A. Ahlberg, *Please Mrs Butler*. London: Puffin. pp. 16–17.

Allen, R. (2016) 'School suspensions are an adult behaviour' [video], *TEDx talk*. www.rosemarieallen.com/videos-.html (accessed March 26, 2021).

Bombèr, L.M. (2007) *Inside I'm Hurting: Practical Strategies for Supporting Children with Attachment Difficulties in Schools*. Belper: Worth.

Brewster, T. and Louallen, S. (2016) 'What is Restorative Justice/Restorative Practices?', *Peer Connect*, June 6. https://medium.com/future-of-school/what-is-restorative-justice-restorative-practices-24dbcfa337d5 (accessed March 26, 2021).

Brown, A.M. (2019) *Pleasure Activism: The Politics of Feeling Good*. Chico, CA: AK Press.

Burke Harris, N. (2014) 'How childhood trauma affects health across a lifetime' [video], *TEDMED talk*, September 2014. https://www.ted.com/talks/nadine_burke_harris_how_childhood_trauma_affects_health_across_a_lifetime (accessed March 26, 2021).

Casey, B.J. (2013) 'The teenage brain: An overview', *Current Directions in Psychological Science*, 22 (2): 80–1. doi.org/10.1177/0963721413486971

Casey, B.J. and Caudle, K. (2013) 'The teenage brain: Self control', *Current Directions in Psychological Science*, 22 (2): 82–7. doi.org/10.1177/0963721413480170

Coleman, A. (2019) 'What's intersectionality? Let these scholars explain', *Time Magazine*, March 29. https://time.com/5560575/intersectionality-theory/ (accessed March 26, 2021).

Cowley, S. (2001) *Getting the Buggers to Behave*. London: Continuum.

Dellenty, S. (2010) *Celebrating Difference: A Whole-School Apprach to LGBT+ Inclusion*. London: Bloomsbury.

Dix, P. (2017) *When the Adults Change Everything Changes: Seismic Shifts in School Behaviour*. Carmarthen: Independent Thinking Press.

Durkin, E. and Benwell, M. (2019) 'These 25 Republicans – all white men – just voted to ban abortion in Alabama', *The Guardian*, May 15. https://www.theguardian.com/us-news/2019/may/14/alabama-abortion-ban-white-men-republicans (accessed March 26, 2021).

Evans, K., Hoyle, T., Roberts, F. and Yusuf, B. (2021) *The Big Book of Whole School Wellbeing*. London: Corwin.

Frances-White, D. (2018) *The Guilty Feminist: From Our Noble Goals to Our Worst Hypocrisies*. London: Virago.

Gilchrist, G. (2020) 'An Ecological Approach to School Development', *School Leadership – a Scottish Perspective*, May 21. http://gg1952.blogspot.com/2020/05/an-ecological-approach-to-school.html (accessed March 26, 2021).

Gill, K., Quilter-Pinner, H. and Swift, D. (2017) 'Making the difference: Breaking the link between school exclusion and social exclusion', *IPPR*, October 10. https://www.ippr.org/publications/making-the-difference (accessed March 26, 2021).

Golding, K. (2015) 'Connection before correction: Supporting parents to meet the challenges of parenting children who have been traumatised within their early parenting environments', *Children Australia*, 40: 1–8. doi.org/10.1017/cha.2015.9

Gregory, M. (2020) 'What does the "still face" experiment teach us about connection?', *PsychHelp*. https://psychhelp.com.au/what-does-the-still-face-experiment-teach-us-about-connection/ (accessed March 26, 2021).

Griffiths, J. (2014) *Kith: The Riddle of the Childscape*. London: Hamish Hamilton.

Handa, A. (2019) *The only useful part of BAME is the 'and'*, Foluke Africa. https://folukeafrica.com/the-only-acceptable-part-of-bame-is-the-and/?fbclid=IwAR0-3aD9N_JYjfxp3RgeBlQiw_4XxgbB-OtA7NAL_16KbZ-ZJB3h8sn4zNw (accessed 27th April 2021).

Handa, A. (2020) *Setting Boundaries: Effective, Authentic Communication*, Inspiring Women Changemakers. www.inspiringwomenchangemakers.co.uk/wp-content/uploads/2020/04/Setting-Boundaries.pdf (accessed March 26, 2021).

Henshaw, P. (2017) 'Thirty five children a day are being permanently excluded', *SecEd*, October 11. www.sec-ed.co.uk/news/thirty-five-children-a-day-are-being-permanently-excluded/ (accessed March 26, 2021).

Henshaw, P. (2020) 'The SecEd Podcast: Relationships, sex & health education in schools', *SecEd*, November 18. www.sec-ed.co.uk/knowledge-bank/the-seced-podcast-relationships-sex-health-education-in-schools-relationships-sex-rse-curriculum-teaching-pshe-pastoral-learning-pedagogy-lockdown-lgbt-wellbeing/ (accessed March 26, 2021).

Kell, E. (2018) *How to Survive in Teaching: Without Imploding, Exploding or Walking Away*. London: Bloomsbury.

Klein, R. (2000) *Defying Disaffection: How Schools Are Winning The Hearts and Minds of Reluctant Students*. Stoke on Trent: Trentham.

Lambrakis-Haddad, F. (2020) 'What is trauma?' *Trauma Inform*. www.traumainform.com/what-is-trauma (accessed 14 April 2021).

Mannion, J. and McAllister, K. (2020) *Fear Is the Mind Killer: Why Learning to Learn Deserves Lesson Time - And How to Make It Work for Your Pupils*. Woodbridge: Melton.

McDermott, V. (2017) *We Must Say No to the Status Quo*. London: Corwin.

McIntosh, P. (1998) *White Privilege and Male Privilege* (Working Paper 189). Wellesley, MA: Wellesley Centers for Women. www.wcwonline.org/images/pdf/White_Privilege_and_Male_Privilege_Personal_Account-Peggy_McIntosh.pdf (accessed March 26, 2021).

Moore, C. (2020a) 'The P in PACE: Playfulness', *Ed Psych Insight*, January 27. www.epinsight.com/post/the-p-in-pace-playfulness (accessed March 26, 2021).

Moore, C. (2020b) 'The A in PACE: Acceptance', *Ed Psych Insight*, February 3. www.epinsight.com/post/the-a-in-pace-acceptance (accessed March 26, 2021).

Moore, C. (2020c) 'The C in PACE: Curiosity', *Ed Psych Insight*, February 10. www.epinsight.com/post/the-c-in-pace-curiosity (accessed March 26, 2021).

Moore, C. (2020d) 'The E in PACE: Empathy', *Ed Psych Insight*, February 17. www.epinsight.com/post/the-e-in-pace-empathy (accessed March 26, 2021).

Music, G. (2019) *Nurturing Children: From Trauma to Growth Using Attachment Theory, Psychoanalysis and Neurobiology*. Abingdon: Routledge.

NHS (2018) 'Stages of puberty: What happens to boys and girls', 16 November. www.nhs.uk/live-well/sexual-health/stages-of-puberty-what-happens-to-boys-and-girls/ (accessed March 26, 2021).

O'Brien, J. (2016) *Don't Send Him in Tomorrow: Shining a Light on the Marginalised, Disenfranchised and Forgotten Children of Today's Schools*. Carmarthen: Independent Thinking.

Paradigm (2021) 'A teen's brain isn't fully developed until the age of 25'. https://paradigmtreatment.com/teens-brain-fully-developed-age/ (accessed 29th April 2021).

Perryman, J. and Calvert, G. (2020) 'What motivates people to teach, and why do they leave? Accountability, performativity and teacher retention', *British Journal of Educational Studies*, 68 (1): 3–23. doi: 10.1080/00071005.2019.1589417

Pope, A. and Wurlitzer, S.H. (2017) *Wild Power: Discover the Magic of Your Menstrual Cycle and Awaken the Feminine Path to Power*. London: Hay House.

Restorative Justice Council (2011) *Restorative Justice in Schools Briefing*. https://restorativejustice.org.uk/sites/default/files/files/fbns_rjc_schools_briefing_december_2011.pdf (accessed March 26, 2021).

Roberts, H. (2012) *Oops! Helping Children Learn Accidentally*. Carmarthen: Independent Thinking.

Shanker, S. (n.d.) 'What is self-reg?' *The Merhit Centre*. https://self-reg.ca/self-reg-101/ (accessed March 26, 2021).

Siegel, D.J. (2014a) 'Dan Siegel: The purpose of the teenage brain' [video], *Greater Good Science Center Youtube Channel*, July 22. www.youtube.com/watch?v=gw9GrgNcYcg (accessed March 26, 2021).

Siegel, D.J. (2014b) 'The remodeling brain: Pruning and myelination' [video], *Dr. Dan Siegel Youtube Channel*, January 15. www.youtube.com/watch?v=jXnyM0ZuKNU&t=2s (accessed March 26, 2021).

Siegel, D.J. (2016) *Brainstorm: The Purpose and Power of the Teenage Brain*. London: Scribe.

Siegel, D.J. (2018) 'Dan Siegel – The adolescent brain' [video], *randomactsofkindness Youtube Channel*, November 5. www.youtube.com/watch?v=0O1u5OEc5eY (accessed March 26, 2021).

Solihull Approach (2013) *Info for Parents: Teenage Brain Development*. www.merseycare.nhs.uk/media/4628/Teenage-Brain-Development-Information.pdf (accessed 29th April 2021).

Souers, K. with Hall, P. (2016) *Fostering Resilient Learners: Strategies For Creating a Trauma-Sensitive Classroom*. Alexandria, VA: ASCD Publishers.

Stonewall (2018) 'LGBT facts and figures 2018'. www.stonewall.org.uk/media/lgbt-facts-and-figures (accessed March 26, 2021).

Team Teach (2021) 'Team Teach – about us'. www.teamteach.co.uk/about-us/ (accessed March 26, 2021).

TES (2021) 'More than 1 in 3 teachers plan to leave by 2026', April 8. www.tes.com/news/covid-schools-workload-more-1-3-teachers-plan-leave-2026 (accessed May 21, 2021).

Thompson, F. and Smith, P.K. (2010) *The Use and Effectiveness of Anti-Bullying Strategies in Schools*, Department of Education. https://assets.publishing.service.gov.uk/government/uploads/system/uploads/attachment_data/file/182421/DFE-RR098.pdf (accessed March 26, 2021).

Timpson, E. (2019) *Timpson Report on School Exclusions*, Department of Education. https://assets.publishing.service.gov.uk/government/uploads/system/uploads/attachment_data/file/807862/Timpson_review.pdf (accessed March 26, 2021).

Tomlinson-Gray, D. (ed.) (2021) *Big Gay Adventures in Education: Supporting LGBT+ Visibility and Inclusion in Schools*. Abingdon: Routledge.

Twist, L. (2014) 'What you appreciates appreciates', *The Chopra Centre*, August 7. https://chopra.com/articles/what-you-appreciate-appreciates (accessed March 26, 2021).

World Health Organization (2021) *Adolescent and Young Adult Health*. www.who.int/news-room/fact-sheets/detail/adolescents-health-risks-and-solutions (accessed 30th April 2021).

Wright, E. (2020) 'Infantilising disabled people is a thing and you're probably unconsciously doing it', *Medium*, January 13. https://medium.com/age-of-awareness/infantilising-disabled-people-is-a-thing-and-youre-probably-unconsciously-doing-it-1adf91dc0fc5 (accessed March 26, 2021).

INDEX